DARREN MCGARVEY aka LOKI grew up in Pollok. He is a writer, performer, columnist and former rapper-in-residence at Police Scotland's Violence Reduction Unit. He has presented eight programmes for BBC Scotland exploring the root causes of anti-social behaviour and social deprivation.

Praise for *Poverty Safari*:

'A blistering analysis of the issues facing the voiceless and the social mechanisms that hobble progress, all wrapped up in an unput-downable memoir.'—DENISE MINA

'Another cry of anger from a working class that feels the pain of a rotten, failing system. Its value lies in the strength it will add to the movement for change.'—KEN LOACH

'Raw, powerful and challenging.'—KEZIA DUGDALE

'*Poverty Safari* is one of the best accounts of working-class life I have read. A scan of the injuries poverty leaves in Britain, which manages to be humane, angry and wise all at the same time. McGarvey is a rarity: a working-class writer who has fought to make the middle-class world hear what he has to say.'—NICK COHEN, THE GUARDIAN

Liason Co-ordinator

efturryd geenuz iz speel
iboot whut wuz right
nwhut wuz rang
boot this nthat
nthi nix thing

a sayzti thi bloke
nwhut izzit yi caw
yir joab jimmy

am a liason co-ordinator
hi sayz oh good ah sayz
a liason co-ordinator

jist whut this erria needs
whut way aw thi unimploymint
inaw thi bevvyin
nthi boayz runnin amock
nthi hoossyz fawnty bits
nthi wummin n tranquilisers
it last thiv sent uz
a liason co-ordinator

sumdy wia digree
in fuck knows whut
getn peyd fur no known
whut thi fuck ti day way it

Tom Leonard

Poverty Safari

Understanding the Anger of Britain's Underclass

DARREN McGARVEY

Luath Press Limited

EDINBURGH

www.luath.co.uk

This book is dedicated to my beautiful and fragile siblings, Sarah Louise, Paul, Lauren and Stephen. Encoded in this book is everything I've learned about life in 33 years. I'm sorry for the times I wasn't around and for any time you've felt let down by me or anybody else. I love you and look forward to the day we can sit around a table again as a family.

ps: Don't do drugs

First published 2017
Reprinted 2017 (twice)

ISBN: 978-1-912147-03-8

The paper used in this book is recyclable. It is made from low chlorine pulps produced in a low energy, low emission manner from renewable forests.

Printed and bound by
Norhaven, Viborg

Typeset in 10.5 point Sabon by Main Point Books, Edinburgh

Contents

Acknowledgements

If not for the kindness, patience and good faith of others, not least the support and encouragement of my partner, Rebecca, this book would have been impossible to complete. The final push required me to take a couple of weeks away from home, leaving her with much to deal with at a time of considerable upheaval in our lives. Thankfully we have a lot of support, particularly from Linda and Edward Wallace, her loving parents, as well as the rest of her family, who are a source of constant support. I don't know what we would do without you. Thank you for your kindness and your example. I also thank Auntie Rosie and my sister Sarah Louise, who are the glue that holds our family together; and Uncle Thomas, for always being there with the heavy lifting. Thank you all for teaching me how to be useful, as well as opinionated. Your support never goes unnoticed.

To my close friends, who I don't see as often as I would like – I always write with you in mind. Once we clear the wreckage of our 20s, we'll hopefully find new ways to be with each other without Lady Carnage looking over our shoulder.

Acknowledgement must go to David Burnett aka Big Div, the first person to recognise and nurture my talents when I was a wayward young person; Hip Hop has given me the opportunity to live an extraordinary life and much of what I have achieved can be traced back to those early days in Ferguslie Park. Thanks also to Sace Lockhart and David 'Defy' Roberts, for being the big brothers I never had and for supporting me throughout my life.

Special thanks to Gavin at Luath Press for trusting my vision and for being intuitive to my needs as a budding (I want to say young) author. Also to Jennie Renton for her input towards the end of the editorial process (I wince at the thought of what I was prepared to release prior to her involvement), and to Hilary Bell, who was a great support at the outset when I had no clue what I was doing.

Many thanks also to Neu! Reekie! for being one of the few safe spaces currently open to me in the Scottish cultural landscape. Much of what ended up in this book came from explorations I was encouraged to embark on at Neu! Reekie! events – it's nice when people introduce you without apologising for you in advance. Thanks are also due to the editors, directors, journos, professionals and mentors whose support, guidance and constructive criticism have been fundamental in the progression of my writing, in particular, Mike Small, Paul McNamee, Claire Stewart, Stephen Daisley and Karyn, Graham and June at the VRU. I also wish to thank my college lecturers, Kathleen, Felicity, Karen, Mary and Charles, for teaching me the difference between opinion and journalism, and my long-suffering classmates, especially Cat, Conor and Anna-Roisin, who got me through the course after a bad relapse into drinking.

I feel grateful to the Scottish writers and performers, professional or otherwise, who have been a source of inspiration and support to me, in different ways, and in particular, Tom Leonard. Deep thanks are due for his encouragement, wisdom and sincerity – and for re-minding me exactly what I'm up against as an aspiring writer from Pollok. I also thank him for giving permission for me to include his poem 'Liason Coordinator', originally published in *Ghostie Men*.

A tip of the cap to the Poverty Truth Commission, class of 2009 – the original and best. Our time together fundamentally changed the direction of my thinking and, thus, of my life. I hope I've written a book that reflects our hopes, fears, dilemmas and contradictions. Special thanks to Paul Chapman for his thoughtfulness and com-passion; when people ask me if I am a man of faith, I still say the same thing: 'Do I really have a choice?' On that note, thank you to my sponsor, James, for showing me a new way to live. None of this would be possible without sobriety.

This book was also made possible thanks to the donations of 228 people, whose support me through a crowdfunded appeal allowed me to focus on writing for a year, knowing that my family would not be adversely affected and, crucially, that I did not have to justify myself to anyone. I am grateful to all of you for affording me the time and space to write *Poverty Safari* – your support has been a point of light in moments when my confidence has dimmed, allowing me to find my way through a thick wood of self-doubt while embarking on my first year of fatherhood – my son, Daniel, being the greatest gift of all.

Finally, thank you to my father, who always believed I could be a writer. You might be right. X

Darren McGarvey, July 2017

Preface

THIS BOOK, WHICH began as a side project to my work as a rapper and columnist, slowly consumed every waking moment of my life until eventually I had to draw down or stop all my other commitments to get it finished. It has taken over a year and a half to complete. On 14 June 2017, two days before my final deadline, I awoke to news of a fire in a tower block in west London.

Like everyone, I was shocked, horrified and devastated by the images. As the morning progressed, more news emerged from the now smouldering shell of Grenfell Tower. We heard stories of people being trapped on the upper floors, forced to throw young children from the building before being consumed by the flames themselves. Then there were the tales of heroism and sacrifice, of people who ran into the building to alert their sleeping neighbours with no regard for their own safety. I kept thinking about the phones that must have been ringing in the pockets of the dead.

Later that day, we learned of the farewell messages posted on social media from victims who knew they were about to die. My eyes filled with tears at their courage in such hopeless circumstances. Trapped within the envelope of smoke and flame that had engulfed their homes as they slept, these brave souls faced their final moments with incredible dignity. I thought of my own son and imagined having to choose between throwing him out of a window on the slight chance he would survive, and keeping him in my arms until the flames consumed us. Just contemplating such a choice is terrible enough. Residents in Grenfell were forced to make these decisions.

This ferocious blaze, which started in one flat before leaping up and around the entire building, was not caused by someone looking to inflict harm. This fireball was not a consequence of a terrorist act. This inferno was a preventable disaster; a confluence of human error and industrial-scale negligence. In the days that followed, the United Kingdom, already destabilised following an election result that had

severely weakened central government, stood on the very cliff-edge of
civil unrest. Prime Minister Theresa May, accused of poor leadership
in response to the fire, was bundled into a car after being jeered by
locals in Grenfell. The news coverage showed a deeply traumatised
community attempting to reorganise itself in a leadership vacuum.
On the ground, the authorities struggled to respond to the crisis.
There was confusion as to how victims could access support and
uncertainty about the number of dead. The local authority, much
like the national government, was failing to perform its most basic
functions.

In the absence of any concrete information, angry, grief-stricken
members of the community began filling the void with speculation
and recrimination. When crowds gathered to make their presence felt
at Kensington and Chelsea Borough Council headquarters, officials
retreated behind the scenes to their very own Forbidden City where
they remained concealed, out of public view, like all the mechanisms
of power in this community. Despite talk of riots, the people of
Grenfell behaved in exemplary fashion. A week after the fire, as the
death toll climbed, survivors were still sleeping in cars or in public
parks.

The extent to which the voices of the Grenfell community had been
routinely ignored played a key role in the sequence of decisions that
led to the fire, not least the choice, made in the name of cost-saving,
of flammable cladding and insulation materials that encouraged the
fire's rapid, deadly spread through the building.

> The materials proposed will provide the building with a fresh
> appearance that will not be harmful to the area or views around
> it. Due to its height the tower is visible from the adjacent
> Avondale Conservation Area to the south and the Ladbroke
> Conservation Area to the east. The changes to the existing
> tower will improve its appearance especially when viewed
> from the surrounding area. Therefore views into and out of the
> conservation areas will be improved by the proposals.

> Planning Application, 2014, for the refurbishment of Grenfell Tower

I feel a strong sense of connection to the people of Grenfell. I know
the hustle and bustle of high-rise life, the dark and dirty stairwells,
the temperamental elevators that smell like urine and wet dog fur, the
grumpy concierge, the apprehension you feel as you enter or leave

the building, especially at night. I know that sense of being cut off from the world, despite having such a wonderful view of it through a window in the sky; that feeling of isolation, despite being surrounded by hundreds of other people above, below and either side of you. But most of all, I understand the sense that you are invisible, despite the fact that your community can be seen for miles around and is one of the most prominent features of the city skyline.

The community around Grenfell Tower is like many with which I am familiar: communities regarded as 'deprived', where there is a pathological suspicion of outsiders and of the authorities; where there is a deeply ingrained belief that there is no point in participating in the democratic process because people in power do not care about the concerns of the 'underclass'.

What really struck a nerve was the news that locals had been warning about the safety of Grenfell Tower for years, and the knowledge that the fire had been avoidable. By midday on the day of the blaze I had discovered the Grenfell Action Group blog where scores of detailed articles, covering a broad range of complex community issues, had been published. I discovered that residents had specifically warned of the fire risk because of the inadequacy of fire safety procedures, and had questioned the 'stay put' instruction which came to national attention following the blaze. Disturbingly, the blog had foreseen that it would take a catastrophic loss of life before attention was paid to the situation.

As the days passed, a window opened up into Grenfell and by proxy, into the lives of the underclass. Countless newspaper articles, bulletins and radio programmes attempted to capture what it was like to live in a tower block. Having been ignored – and dismissed – for so long, now suddenly everybody was interested in what life in a community like this entailed. But most people, despite their noble intentions, were just passing through on a short-lived expedition. A safari of sorts, where the indigenous population is surveyed from a safe distance for a time, before the window on the community closes and everyone gradually forgets about it.

This is a pattern I have seen repeated in my own community for as long as I can remember, and so my intention has been for *Poverty Safari* to resonate with people who feel misunderstood and unheard, that the book might be a sort of forum, giving voice to their feelings and concerns. The themes and issues explored here are clearly pertinent to those communities – like Grenfell – where people are routinely ignored by decision-makers who think they know better, even when they are fatally mistaken. What I explore here might lend context to the outpouring of rage that followed the Grenfell Tower fire and, crucially, an understanding that this rage is not just about the fire and tragic loss of life. In communities all over Britain where people experience multiple levels of deprivation in health, housing and education and are effectively politically excluded, anger is felt. And this anger is something we will all have to get used to, unless things change. In *Poverty Safari*, drawing from my own experience and expressing my own political perspective, I have attempted to set out what some of that change might look like.

Introduction

PEOPLE LIKE ME don't write books – or so my head keeps telling me. 'Write a book?' it sneers over my shoulder, 'you haven't read enough of them to even attempt such a thing.' It's true. I am not a habitual reader of books though I am a regular consumer of words. Since my schooldays, how words look, sound and what they mean has been my primary interest. As a child I was keen to engage grown-ups in conversation, always trying to collect new words to add to my growing vocabulary. I'm told that by the age of five I was precociously correcting my mother's terrible grammar, much to her annoyance. By the time I was ten, I was formulating my first short stories, borrowing heavily, as one does, from my main influences at the time: Granny and Batman.

But I don't remember reading any books. I do recall occasionally picking them up and flicking through a few pages, or delving for a specific piece of information, such as the capital city of Turkey – which is not Istanbul. I don't remember the moment so many people speak of, when they finish the life-changing book that ignites their passion for reading. I do, however, retain vivid memories of struggling with books and being intimidated by their physical size and word-count. Just the thought of a big book was enough to defeat me.

In secondary school, when my ability to write put me in the top English class, I was out of my depth when it came to literature. People would tell me I just hadn't found the right book, that I should persevere. They insisted that all I had to do was work my brain like a muscle until reading became less of a chore. But I secretly resented this advice – and those who dispensed it. Instead, I settled on the belief that there was some unseen barrier preventing me from connecting with literature. It's not as if I was the only one at my school who struggled. Regular readers were the exception. Reading was not regarded as a leisure activity, more a necessary evil, something to be endured. Where I diverged from many of my classmates was that I privately longed to read every book I picked up. However, to my frustration and later, resignation, I always found, not long after starting one, that I could never see it through.

Lightweight paperbacks were deceptively small, often luring me in with an interesting cover, but I'd quickly return them to the shelf when I discovered the absence of illustrations. Those books were so crammed with words that they appeared cluttered and chaotic to my eye – filling me with the sort of dread an imminent house move triggers when you think about it for too long. Tiny lettering, coupled with tight paragraph spacing, provoked a sense of impossibility that only got worse as time went on. Only a few pages into *Lord of the Rings* and I was demoralised. I was always being told about Frodo's famous quest across Middle-earth. I'm ashamed to admit that I always had to nip off before the end of Bilbo's party.

Hardback books appeared much easier to read because the letters were bigger, but I found their bulk and weight off-putting. My English teacher insisted that I read and review John Irving's *A Prayer for Owen Meany* for my Higher English qualification. It was nice to know he thought me capable of such a feat (with a 617-page novel!) but his generosity wasn't enough to stop me from baulking violently at the idea. It was a misreading of my abilities, akin to sending a toddler up a mountain. We compromised on Tennessee Williams' *A Streetcar Named Desire*, which I found less challenging because it was a playscript and therefore appeared less messy on the page. There was the additional benefit of having a film version to turn to when my stamina began to wane.

For me, multi-volume sagas like Harry Potter were out of the question. If I had to take part in a discussion about, say, Roald Dahl's *Fantastic Mr Fox* or Anne Fine's *Flour Babies*, I could glean enough information from bite-size portions to feign that I had read the book in its entirety.

I was still imbibing a lot of new words, increasingly from newspapers, but I came to depend on listening to other people discuss and debate as a way of grasping what I might otherwise have learned from a book. Which is how I became interested in understanding opposing points of view and started scrutinising my own beliefs and those of the people around me, sometimes to their annoyance.

I preferred taking in information that I could interact with. Discussion was more engaging and fun, and was not an endurance test like reading. By talking and listening to what others had to say and paying attention to how they said it, I developed an ability to communicate with different types of people on a broad range of subjects, which might even have suggested I was an avid reader. The act of reading, and indeed all forms of academic achievement, were regarded by many of my male peers as either feminine or the preserve of posh people and freaks. Had I attended secondary school in a community where being smart was more socially acceptable, perhaps I would have been a better reader.

In poetry, I found only frustration and confusion. It wasn't just the opaque metaphors and bizarre punctuation, but also the subject matter. These poems were couched in such high language that they seemed to sneer down their noses at me. I was sceptical that anyone could understand or enjoy it. My struggle to find meaning – or rather, my struggle to find the meaning ascribed by the curriculum, in order that I pass a test – led me to take an increasingly hostile and suspicious attitude towards poetry and poets, which matched my now belligerent attitude towards reading and readers. However, beneath my disruptive behaviour lay an aggrieved sense of rejection and exclusion, and a crushing feeling of personal failure. The realm of print felt so impossibly exclusive that I developed a fear and anxiety around books despite my interest in their main ingredient: words. At some point, I made the decision that big books were for certain types of people who went to fancy schools, lived in fancy houses, spoke in fancy accents and ate fancy food.

This was a false belief.

Then, of course, having integrated a false belief into my sense of identity, I had to create reasons to explain why it was true. It wouldn't do to accept that reading or, for that matter, concentrating was beyond me, or to accept that I required extra support and should ask for it – especially since I was getting reasonable grades for the writing I was turning in. I was therefore, due to my own stubbornness, caught between a prideful pretension that I was intelligent and the humbling reality that I couldn't read a book.

But rather than be humbled, I began to construct an elaborate, grandiose yarn to explain it. My inability to finish a book was not a sign of a lack of intelligence, but a testament to my independent mindedness. I couldn't read a book because the books I was being asked to read, that I was told were good, were, in fact, rubbish. I couldn't read a book because the curriculum was full of pretentious, upper class nonsense that said nothing about my community or experience. I came to believe these works were being imposed on me and that my value as a person was being derived from an ability to memorise and repeat a series of cultural prompts and cues from teachers. Teachers who themselves had ascended into positions of authority by doing the same.

Perhaps there was a kernel of truth to that belief. However, I had no insight into why I adopted it in the first place. It was not, as I then believed, about critical thinking or independent mind-edness. It was primarily about deflecting attention from my own inadequacies and shortcomings. I'd have been deeply offended had you told me that back then. In my frustration at not being able to read a book and the sense of exclusion this instilled in me, I adopted a world view that would place me at odds with nearly every person, place and thing I'd encounter. I stayed that way until one morning, many years later, when I woke up drunk in a police cell and realised my life had to change radically.

I've read many books, often not the way you're supposed to read them. I suspect this will be reflected in how I think and write. The idea that people like me don't write books rings in my ears. Perhaps what I have composed is a series of loosely connected rants that give the appearance of a book, much in the same way I give the appearance of a reader. I attempt to express many things here, including my unconventional reading habits. I've tried to write for people like me who struggle with reading, and invite them to feel free to dip in and out at random, read bits and pieces in the wrong order, or go for shorter chapters individually. At the same time, I have remained true to myself in how I think, speak and write, and deploy the full range of my vocabulary, the words I have collected throughout my life.

I know greater books than this have been written about poverty. I just haven't read any.

Crime and Punishment

THE WOMEN ENTER the performing arts space in single file wearing purple jackets and grey jogging bottoms. It's important to greet them confidently; making eye contact and offering a handshake though careful not to acknowledge too overtly if that offer is declined. As the last of a quintet enters the space, the door is locked quickly behind her by the tall, burly man in uniform who accompanied them here moments before. Satisfied that the space is secure, he joins his colleague in a control room at the back and I invite the women to a seating area, arranged in a circle in front of a blank flipchart.

The performing arts centre, deep in the heart of the prison, is a sight to behold. A fully functioning theatre, rehearsal space and performance venue, it can be used for workshops, seminars and film screenings. The space is cool and dark, which is striking when you first enter, given how starkly it contrasts with the rest of the building which, depending on your location, is either grey or white. In a corner there's a selection of musical instruments, the most popular being the acoustic guitar. Above the small elevated stage in the front and centre of the room a modest lighting rig hovers above a multi-speaker sound system. This is as good a set-up as I've seen in a public institution. Usually, equipment of this scope and specification would have to be hired in but for obvious reasons that is impractical in this case; the moment you enter the prison at the main gate, it feels like going through customs. Even staff who work here every day must go through the same security checks when they enter and leave. For freelancers like me, this experience can be unsettling and intimidating – especially if you've had dealings with the police or been through the court system. Arriving at the performing arts space provides relief from the palpable tension of this oppressive and potentially hostile environment, though it must be said that it only takes a couple of visits in quick succession before you adjust and it begins to feel normal. I suspect many of the women who have signed up for today's rap workshop only did so because it meant they could come here. In the context of the prison, this is something of an oasis and if the performing arts space was the only part of the facility you ever visited, you'd be forgiven for doubting whether you were in a prison at all.

Following some small talk, which consists of making basic observations about the space, I attempt to make a proper start to proceedings though, admittedly, I am feeling a little unsure of myself.

'Why do you think I'm here?' I ask. In other circumstances, I've found this question to be an effective opening gambit because, while appearing vague and almost too simple, it performs many important functions at once. For one thing, it immediately removes the onus from me, which is convenient because I haven't properly prepared. Or rather, I've underestimated how startled I would feel, caught in the headlights of an unfamiliar audience. Unprepared and feeling out of my depth, I am about to fluff what should be a simple introduction.

The question 'Why am I here?' buys me a few minutes to get my bearings and settle my nerves while concealing both my lack of preparation as well as slight anxiety. However, it serves another function, far more useful than simply saving my skin, which is why I've come to depend on it so much. The question 'Why am I here?', should people engage with it, creates the potential for interactions that may help me get to know the participants much quicker. By observing these interactions, it's possible to get a better handle on their personality types, abilities, communication skills and learning patterns, as well as a sense of the hierarchy within the group. The quotation gives me a chance to tease out exactly what expectations they have of me – if any.

This facility is a young offenders' institution for around 830 young men though the actual population is higher than that. Most of the inmates are between the ages of 16 and 21. The inmates, or YOS as they are often referred to by professionals, are segregated along lines of age and the nature of their crime. There's also a section of the prison population here on remand, meaning they are due to appear in court to be sentenced but have been deemed unsuitable for release by a judge. This group are marked by a different colour of t-shirt, usually red. Everyone else wears dark blue. Then there's the sex offenders who, along with those in 'protection', are segregated from the rest of the prison population. Those in protection have been placed there for their own safety. This is usually because a threat has been made against them, or they believe themselves to be in danger, or they have been branded a 'grass'. People are put in protection for many reasons but because they are lumped in with the sex offenders, by extension, they are also deemed 'beasts', 'paedos' and 'wrong yins'. In here people don't make distinctions between grasses and sex offenders. For many of the young men, 'not grassing' is what constitutes their moral compass. For some, no crime is quite as shameful as giving information to police that results in someone else's criminal conviction.

Lack of space due to a steady increase in the overall prison population means that many young men on short term sentences for less serious offences, such as drug possession or shoplifting, are placed in the same halls as the more serious violent offenders, many of whom are serving long term sentences for murder – or botched attempts at it. The effect of this cross-pollination of violent criminals and non-violent criminals is simply the potential for more violence, which is acute in every corner of the prison. Funnily enough, the sex offenders are the least aggressive and most cooperative group and the contrast between them and everyone else is quite striking.

In this environment, the tiniest dispute can quickly escalate into an explosive act. Intended as a place of rehabilitation – as well as punishment – prison is by far the most violent place in society. The violence is so tangible that you cannot inhabit this place for very long without being altered or deformed by it in some way, which is why people tend to adjust to it quickly. Some adjust by becoming more aggressive and violent, others by taking drugs like Valium, heroin, or, more recently, spice. But the ubiquity of violence is not as startling to the prisoner as it is to people who only visit occasionally. This frightening tinderbox atmosphere is mirrored in the communities and households many of these prisoners grew up in, where acts of violence are so frequent that people become desensitised to them, discussing incidents jovially, much in the same way people talk about the weather.

A few months ago, someone's face was slashed in the prison cafeteria over a dispute about a piece of toast. In this hostile social climate, violence is often not only a practical demonstration of brute force, but often a form of communication. Should a person be seen to back down from one confrontation, they will often become subject to more threats and attacks from people who sense their vulnerability. Slashing someone over a bit of toast may appear brutal, mindless and barbaric, but in a twisted way it may also be an attempt to reduce the threat of violence further down the line. People are unlikely to mess with the guy who will slash you over a piece of toast and this rationale, which is pathological in violent communities, is as much about survival as it is about pride or reputation. In fact, pride and bravado are often just a social extension of a deeper survival instinct. Regardless of the context of the violence, its function is often the same; it's not just practical but performative and designed to ward off potential aggressors as well as eliminating a direct threat. Not everyone who comes here is violent but it's hard not to get drawn into the culture of violence once you arrive. It's often the case that people leave prison far more violent than when they arrived. This also applies to drug problems, which often escalate once the reality of prison life sets in.

Generally speaking, women are less violent. This morning's group were recently relocated here following the closure of Scotland's only all-female prison, Cornton Vale, that ran at a cost of

£12m a year and was home to around 400 female cons and young offenders. In 2006, 98 per cent of the inmates in Cornton Vale had addiction issues while 80 per cent had problems with mental health; 75 per cent were survivors of abuse.

But while their new home, here in the young offenders' institution is, primarily, for the rehabilitation of young men, these women are adults. Some of them have children of their own who, on the outside, live under the care of relatives or public institutions. Perhaps that's what a couple of them are thinking about as they stare blankly into space, baffled by my open-ended question.

Admittedly, I've made stronger starts than this. Sometimes, I glide right through this initial pass and have people eating out of the palm of my hand but today, I find myself inhibited by the same self-doubt I can faintly detect in them. I point out that nobody is obligated to respond to the question of why I am here but privately I'm really hoping someone does. Should they take the plunge and be the first to answer, it may tell me something vital about that individual and, thus, something about the group. For example, some people raise their hand before they speak and this may indicate either good manners or submissiveness to authority, depending on the context. Others interject before you've finished asking the question and this may indicate enthusiasm, self-confidence or the need to state clearer boundaries. It's useful not to make too many assumptions about individuals and groups, based on how they behave initially. A serial interrupter may have a hearing problem or a learning difficulty. Obviously, I can't clear my head of all presumption, but what I can choose to observe are those assumptions as they emerge in my mind without acting on them. These assumptions say as much about me as they do about the subject of my judgement.

In the prison environment, when leading a discussion, I try to regard all forms of verbal communication as valid, at least in this early stage. It's important not to impose rules too quickly either – especially if I have not yet established basic facts about who I'm talking to. In these initial moments, what I'm trying to do is build a rapport, based on mutual respect, that will hopefully make it easier for me to negotiate entry into their community. I increase my chances of doing that by acknowledging them as people with agency.

'Why do you think I'm here?' sets a collaborative tone and functions as my statement of intent. Many of these women (and the prison population generally) are accustomed – conditioned even – to being addressed by authority figures who exercise power over them. While this is only right in the prison environment, it's often the case that authority figures, over time, forget to actively listen to those whom they come to regard as inferior, either socially or professionally. A gulf opens up between the professionals and the service users which can become fraught with misunderstanding should anyone attempt to bridge it. That's why people tend to stick to their own and conform to type, whatever side of the divide they may find themselves on.

By starting my workshop with a question, I signal to the group these dynamics have been temporarily suspended. That the usual flow of power has been interrupted. Rather than having all the answers, by virtue of my elevated status, I'm letting them know that without their input, I know nothing at all. The women may also infer that by asking them a question, I'm recognising the value in their experience and insight.

'You're the mad rapper guy,' says a woman with self-inflicted scars up and down her arms.

'We're here to write songs,' says another, in a slow drawl that indicates either methadone or sedative use.

With every response, I begin to build a fuller picture of who and what it is I'm really working with here.

'That's right,' I answer, before asking their names and giving them a bit of background information on me, which I impart, as I always do, in a short rap performance. The song is called 'Jump' and was written specifically to engage groups quickly, which is crucial when working with people who suffer from poor concentration and low self-esteem. The quicker they feel like they know what is going on the better. The faster they feel they have a stake in participating, the less likely they are to revolt or become apathetic. The sooner they get into the book, the harder they'll find it to put down.

Anxiety or fear in relation to an activity or task often presents as either a lazy or adversarial attitude. Over the years, I've learned a few tricks to keep people tuned in. One is to say something positive about them. Every interaction is important because it presents an opportunity to acknowledge or reaffirm something about the participant. This works even better if you acknowledge something they already do well; skills or personality traits which they already possess and do not need to acquire from someone else. It's harder to disengage when you feel like you have something to lose. Complimenting a person's handwriting, their sense of humour or an interesting observation or turn of phrase can go a long way. If someone is quiet, maybe they have an interesting tattoo or great colour coordination in how they dress. These things indicate depth, richness and personal agency that deserve to be remarked upon. In the world of prison, tiny things are massive and just as someone could slash you over a slice of toast, the polarity of someone's day could be reversed by the simple exchange of a kindness:

'You've got really neat handwriting.'

The second you say something positive, whatever it may be, the participant will instinctively deflect it, reinforcing a more familiar negative:

'Me? Neat handwriting? Aye right. I'm stupid. I can't write.'

But if you pay attention, you'll notice that they light up and become bashful at having received a compliment the second they think you aren't looking. On a good day, they may even ponder the compliment in more depth later, and dare to grapple with the possibility that it might be true. These are the tiny interactions that help you and the participants get under one another's skin, creating the chemistry necessary to instil trust and self-confidence within the group.

Participants who face barriers to education such as poor literacy or low self-esteem usually – though not always – come from backgrounds where their abilities are not acknowledged or nurtured, making it harder for them to take risks. For this group, simply reading out loud or expressing an opinion can be daunting and even intimidating, which means you have to remain intuitive to a person's needs if you want to encourage them beyond their comfort zone. For the ones who end up in prison it's often worse; their talents are suppressed, ridiculed or actively discouraged and become a source of embarrassment or shame. This can evolve into a tendency to conceal aspects of self that reveal vulnerability as well as reinforcing a belief that they are stupid. If things seem to drag at the start of a lesson then people disengage, assuming the fault is with them and their lack of intelligence – even if it's really down to an ill-prepared facilitator like me. This core belief that they aren't smart enough often manifests as a disruptive, confrontational or aggressive attitude. The challenging behaviour is used to deflect any interaction that might reveal their fear, sense of inadequacy or vulnerability.

For workshops like this, I usually perform a song as an icebreaker. One of the tracks I do is called 'Jump'. The first line is: 'Growing up, I never knew who to trust, looking at the world though the window of a school bus, gob-stopper in my mouth, I didn't mind school, it got me out the house.'

The lyrics are autobiographical and detail my school years and the sudden death of my mother. But the song is also deliberately laden with the imagery and language of lower class communities, with references to alcohol products like MD 20/20 and Buckfast, and rap artists like Tupac Shakur. Themes of family breakdown, abandonment, alcoholism and bereavement, as well as playful jibes at the middle class and law enforcement, not only reflect their own experiences back at them but, crucially, recognise the validity of those experiences. The song, like much of the culture they engage with, regarded as coarse, offensive or lacking sophistication, appeals to them because it reveals the richness of their own experience; the poetry in what is often regarded by wider society as the dereliction and vulgarity of their lives.

Administering punishment is the role of the state. My job is to help these people express their humanity in an environment where it can get them killed.

Participants, whether in a prison setting or any other setting populated by people from deprived backgrounds, will often scan me while I talk, looking for signs that I can be trusted, that I am 'sound'. They will observe how I speak, which words I use and the dialect in which those words are couched. They will instinctively attempt to ascertain the distance between who I really am and who I say I am. In this environment, authenticity is the yardstick by which all people are measured. That is why you rarely find high status people, speaking in high status language, operating in communities like this – unless they are surrounded by security or imbued with some sort of legal authority. When people come here to work, they often adopt personas that they think will appeal to the participants, forgetting the prison population is filled with some of the most emotionally intuitive and manipulative people you are likely to find.

Although people end up in prison for all sorts of reasons, one common theme for most people behind bars is that they have experienced emotional, psychological, physical or sexual abuse of some sort which – almost always – precedes their criminality. Maltreatment or neglect at the hands of a care-giver appears to play a significant role in triggering the germinal factors that lead to offending behaviour: low self-esteem, poor educational attainment, substance misuse and social exclusion.

Towards the end of the workshop, one woman, who has been quiet until now, casually mentions that both of her parents and her sister recently died after purchasing fake street Valium. Even so, she continues to use the drug in prison. She's here because she took the blame for something her boyfriend did. Despite this, he ended up in here anyway having started using heroin shortly after the murder of his best friend, which he witnessed in his own flat. The dispute was about drugs. She will retell the story of her dead family several times throughout the course of my work with her, almost as if she's forgotten the previous times. On the fourth week, she will shed a tear. She will tell me that this is the first tear

she has shed in front of other people in prison. This is her way
of letting me know that she trusts me. When she begins to sob,
the other women console her with all the care and tenderness of
a nurturing and supportive family, something many of them have
never known.

Many of the people in this prison are repeat offenders. Many
deserve to be here for what they have done. Many have committed crimes against innocent, law-abiding citizens that warrant
punishment. When you work in this environment it's easy to forget about the victims of crime. But while it's crucial to recognise
this, it's also true to say that much of the destructive and socially
harmful behaviour we see from offenders has a definite starting
point. If you take almost anyone in this prison, excluding psycho-
paths and the criminally insane, and dial back their lives to a time
before they were criminals, what you are likely to find is that, as
children, they were the victims of some form of violence.

2

A History of Violence

BY THE AGE of ten I was well adjusted to the threat of violence. In some ways, violence itself was preferable to the threat of violence. When you are being hit – or chased – part of you switches off. You become physically numb as the violent act is carried out. A disassociation occurs. You become detached from the violent act as it is being perpetrated against you. The disassociation can make you physically numb as well as emotionally unresponsive. Your body goes into self-preservation mode until the threat is over. Thankfully, angry people tire easily. Therefore, the key to enduring a violent episode at the hands of someone you can't evade or fight back against, is usually to submit and hope that you don't sustain a serious injury.

Acts of violence are terrifying, but a sustained threat of violence is sometimes much worse. If the violence occurs in the home, then it's something you feel in the air. You adapt to the threat by becoming hypervigilant. This heightened state of awareness is effective in short, sharp doses but when the fear of violence is constant, hypervigilance becomes your default emotional setting, making it very hard to relax or be in the present moment.

In a home where violence, or the threat of violence, is regular, you learn how to negotiate it from a young age. You become adept at reading facial expressions and body language as well as scanning the tone of people's voices to detect and deter possible threats. You become a skilful emotional manipulator, able to keep an abuser's anger at bay by remaining intuitive to their needs and triggers and adjusting your behaviour accordingly. These survival strategies, cobbled together through trial and error, eventually become instinctive. For many people they remain, integrated fully into their personality, long after the threat of violence is gone. However, these strategies only work for so long before they inevitably fail. In addition, by seeking to contort yourself around the needs of the person you're afraid of, you simply prolong the dread that feeds the hypervigilance. Dread, in this context, being a sense of anxious expectation that precedes a violent incident. It's a catch-22. On one hand, you don't want the violence to happen. On the other, you know it is inevitable and would rather just get it out of the way.

One such event occurred when I was about five years old. We had not long moved to the other side of Pollok, where I grew up. Pollok is a so-called deprived area on the southside of Glasgow and in the early '90s it scored high in the tables for social deprivation across Europe. Our new home was a three-bedroom, semi-detached house with a front and back garden. This night, I recall being upstairs in bed but finding it hard to sleep because of noise coming from the living room. My mum had people over and they were downstairs drinking, laughing and listening to music. My next memory is standing at the living room door, before a group of guests. I had my hopes pinned on my mum letting me stay up because she was drunk. I preferred her when she'd had a few drinks. She was much more relaxed, fun and affectionate. But tonight she was having none of it and told me to go back to bed. There was a bit of back-and-forth between us. I suspect I was showing off in front of her guests, probably winding her up or trying to outwit her in some way. Then her tone and posture shifted as she gave me a final warning to go back upstairs. I defied her.

She held my gaze for a moment, before leaping out of her seat and charging into the kitchen. She pulled the cutlery drawer open, reached in and pulled out a long, serrated bread knife. Then she turned round and began pursuing me. I already knew she could be unpredictable but this was like nothing I had witnessed before. I ran out of the room and naively made for the stairs as she emerged from the living room into the hall only seconds behind me. I scrambled up the stairs as fast as I could but she was closing the distance between us. With nowhere to hide I ran into my room, slamming the door behind me, but it just seemed to bounce off her as she came charging through, clutching the knife, like a monster in a nightmare.

If only I had had the sense to run out of the front door instead. Seconds before, she had appeared to be having so much fun that it had felt safe to wind her up in front of people. Now I was trapped in my room, pinned against the wall, with a knife to my throat. I don't remember what she said to me but I do remember the hate in her eyes. I remember thinking that I was about to be cut open and that I would probably die. Just as she lifted the knife to my face, she was pulled from behind and thrown to the other side of the room by my dad, who then restrained her while one of the guests picked me up and bundled me into the back of a car.

I don't remember my mother, or anyone else, ever talking about that night again. Truth be told, I forgot about it myself until many years later, when it came back to me in the form of a flashback.

It's hard to quantify what an experience like that does to a person and even harder to measure the long term impact as life unfolds. All I can say is that events like these, while seeming strangely normal at the time, later found expression in my beliefs about the world and all of the people in it. For if you are not safe in your own home, under the care of your own mother, then where else could you possibly drop your guard?

After explosive incidents like this, whether they involve physical violence or non-physical aggression, there is always the faint hope that the perpetrator's remorse will propel them towards better behaviour. Even when there's no sense of that happening, there remains a perverse allure in their empty promises. In these moments, there is a vulnerability, tenderness and honesty, seen so rarely, that is so affecting that you struggle to resist the twisted logic of your abuser. All you want is for them to love you and this need persists at the expense of your own sanity and safety.

Violence wasn't an everyday thing in our house, but my mother's unpredictability created a chronic sense of dread in me. Sometimes, simply the crime of being upset or scared could get you in trouble. She once threw my bike in the river because I wouldn't stop crying. But while puzzling for me as her son, in the broader context of our community, her drunken, aggressive and violent impulses were not difficult to understand.

In Pollok violence was a part of daily life. Even just a simple trip to the shop around the corner was a risk to your safety – and pride. There were varying degrees of violent threat to consider, from scuffles to proper fighting, and different qualities of violence to fear, such as fist fights or stabbings. What didn't change was the constant awareness of aggression and the potential for it to escalate.

In a community like this, the threat of violence is so pervasive that even when there is no reason to be afraid, the state of hypervigilance keeps you on alert regardless, making daily life considerably stressful. Outside of the home, in the school, violence was more like a public exhibition. People staved off the threat of violence by stoking it up for someone else, whipping the playground into a frenzy until the first blow was struck. Whether at home or in the street, faced with the threat of violence, you will experience the worst possible type of fear. Physically fighting is a horrible, terrifying and dangerous thing to do. I learned early in my life that violence was inevitable and that I had no choice in the matter. So I picked my fights wisely if given the opportunity, earning my stripes in primary school with a boy I fought so many times that eventually people stopped coming to watch.

His house was closer to the school than mine, so I always had to walk past it, which made avoiding him impossible. One day I remember being so exhausted and scared from fighting that I was physically sick. When I did get home, I made the mistake of telling my mum about what had happened. Rather than console me, her response was to grab me by the sleeve of my jacket and march me back down to his house where she would confront his mother and I might be expected to fight again – to prove I wasn't scared. I remember her reacting this way on a few other occasions, sometimes with people who were older than me. One time she marched right into a classroom to threaten a teacher for making me own up to something I didn't do. The trigger that set her off seemed to be me appearing to be frightened by someone. Admitting you were afraid was almost shameful. I like to think, perhaps naively, that her love for me meant the thought of me being frightened or helpless was so upsetting to her that it caused her to overreact. But whatever the cause of her outbursts, it was eclipsed by her desire for retribution. Her solution to the problem of violence was always more violence.

The only reason I ever overcame my fear of the bullies was because it was dwarfed by my fear of my mother. Once she left, the threat of violence remained as I entered my teens and started attending a secondary school where it was present in many forms. Even a couple of the teachers were aggressive and prone to violence. So, much of your thought and energy is given to pretending that you aren't scared of anything whilst simultaneously assessing your safety in relation to a vast array of potential threats throughout the day.

There's no point in fighting someone at the location they stipulate beforehand. They usually choose that location because it gives them a tactical advantage. My biggest worry, when faced with an unavoidable fight, would be that I might gain an early advantage, which could raise the stakes and potentially provoke an extreme act, biting or head kicking. I went into every fight with something to lose. Most of the people I had to fight were not burdened by that anxiety and this gave them a distinct advantage. Their anxiety was like my mother's. Their biggest fear was losing face in front of other people in the community and this gave them an edge. If people were honest, they'd admit that fighting is extremely unpleasant. Sadly, backing down from a confrontation or admitting that you don't want to fight can leave you vulnerable to humiliation as well as more aggression. It's this fear of being ridiculed, cast out or attacked that subtly directs your thinking and behaviour in violent communities.

3

The Call of the Wild

IN THE MIDST of so many potential threats, it's not easy to express yourself – unless you are being aggressive. Most other forms of emotional expression are kept in check, either by mockery or the threat of violence. This makes growing up in a so-called deprived community an oppressive experience. This sense that you are being repressed extends to nearly every means that you have to express your individuality. Which is why nearly everybody dressed and spoke the same. If you didn't conform to the prevailing norm of the day then life became a daily run of the gauntlet.

Just as you'd attract attention for having the gall to wear a pair of trousers with more than two pockets, it became very apparent to other people if you started dropping fancy words into conversation. I recall a summer afternoon, stewing on the school bus as rowdy classmates were being dragged aboard by teachers for the weekly trip to the football pitches. Two minutes on the bus and it was clear the boys were in no mood to behave unpredictably; snarling through their nostrils and homoerotically play-fighting while using the word 'gay' as an adjective for anything that fell outside their frame of reference. By these measures, I was already well out of the closet and that day I made a passing comment about one of the girls in our class, who was sporting an attractive new hairstyle.

'Here, did you see Nicola's new hair? It's fuckin beautiful.'

That sentence might seem uncontroversial, but in this environment, there is a preferred way of speaking. When you are bold enough to speak up amongst a potentially aggressive peer group, it's wise to screen your impending statement in your head beforehand, or you risk inviting a confrontation. Luckily, my sense of what I should and shouldn't say was, by this point, instinctive and I could think on my feet depending on the demands of the situation. If I found myself in a staff room, in the presence of adults with authority, it was natural to take things up a notch and perhaps drop in a reference to politics or current affairs – if there weren't any boys around. For some reason, it always felt natural to alter the way I spoke when conversing with teachers. It was important to me that they knew I was smart. In a school like this, where the threat of mockery and violence hangs in the air, intelligence is an attribute you learn to conceal for reasons of personal safety. Therefore, if the opportunity to flex my intellectual muscle did present itself, it was difficult to pass up.

Not all adults in the school warranted this approach. Topical references to politics or current affairs were less appropriate if you found yourself shooting the breeze with a janitor or a dinner lady. Not because they weren't interested in politics (maybe they were) but simply because they were not the type of people who discussed things of an intellectual nature – or so I gathered.

The janitor's main area of expertise was janitoring. Unless you had a building-related query then there was little to discuss. In our school the janitor was a big man, or fat, as we called him behind his back, and he didn't say very much. When he did it was usually to make you aware of something you were doing wrong. He leered over us and his presence was unpleasant because he seemed to be a deeply unhappy man. If he wasn't scowling by the playground doors at interval, or moving through the school like a glacier, to board up a smashed window or bleed a radiator, he was sitting in his janitorial quarters at the front door, sipping a mug of tea, his long face buried in a tabloid newspaper. Who knows, maybe he was interested in politics? Perhaps he had a burning desire to run in the local council elections? Perhaps the newspaper was concealing a copy of *National Geographic*, to which he devotedly subscribed every month? But there was something about his demeanour, or at least my interpretation of it, that suggested he wasn't up for talking to me about anything. Sometimes he wouldn't even put the paper down to respond to you, he'd just grunt and gesture towards the keys to the toilet.

The dinner ladies were much more welcoming and good-humoured. They gave lunchtime a personal touch and as well as serving your food they would ask how you were getting on. But despite their social skills far exceeding those of the janitor, at no point did it seem appropriate to pick their brains on anything. I found it surreal to see them in some other capacity, like going to the shops or getting off a bus. In my head, they were just the dinner ladies. The idea you could learn anything from anyone but teachers, who possessed the only type of knowledge worth knowing, seemed absurd to me at that time.

If I was talking to a girl, which happened on many occasions, another realm of possibility would open because there would be less pressure to adopt a braggadocio persona. Girls, in most cases, were more mature than boys of a comparable age and I could sense that many of them were exhausted by the unending dither of the males. A conversation with a girl presented the chance to express another side of my personality, the opportunity to liberate myself briefly from the heavy social burdens of the male arena.

As for being trapped on a school bus full of hormonal boys on the way to football, well that was a different story.

Here I couldn't be myself. Here I couldn't be caught thinking about what being myself even meant. My simple desire to express appreciation of an attractive girl's hairstyle was, in fact, not simple at all. Bizarrely, this matter required consideration of the most careful kind. It wouldn't do to simply blurt out the word 'beautiful'. Without some sort of linguistic diversion, or buffer, that would have been too jarring for these boys. New words and ideas filled them with alarm, provoking unpredictable reactions depending on your location and how many of them were present. I knew, intuitively, that using the word 'beautiful' was a risk. That's why I deliberately foreshadowed it with a tougher, coarser word, to soften the blow.

'Here, did you see Nicola's new hair? It's fuckin beautiful.'

Did I really expect my use of an unsanctioned term to go

undetected? As soon as the word passed my lips, silence fell. The boys looked at one another baffled, like primates confronted, for the first time, by a flame. In situations like this no one knew how to respond. Everyone had a sense of how they should respond but no gumption to follow through in case they were rejected by the pack. Some likely agreed with my observation that Nicola's hair was beautiful but were looking to the group for a sign that it was okay to feel this way. Others may have thought it a stupid thing to say, deserving of ridicule, but like the rest, needed reassurance before indicating their position. There may have been at least one who didn't know what the word meant, either mishearing it or perhaps hadn't heard it used by a male before. Despite their reactions being rooted in a desire to project a tough image, they were all terrified to reveal their true thoughts or feelings in that moment. They were anxious to be seen even pondering such things and this fear, which followed them everywhere, was the engine room of much of their behaviour in school – and out.

In absurd scenarios like these, which occurred at least once every day, you could be 'accused' of being gay – like it was a crime – for openly expressing an interest in the opposite sex. Not only that but you could become subject to such a spurious charge by a bunch of boys who weren't happy unless they were writhing around a football field, a rugby scrum or whipping one another's bare arses with towels in a communal shower. But this stupidity dominated the horizon of my every school day from 1996 until 2001. I cannot overstate how I'd dread and loathe those bus journeys, short as they were. Everything about them, much like school itself, was profoundly oppressive. Moment to moment, people were so inhibited by the social expectations of those around them that the simple act of acknowledging reality, in this case a girl's pretty hair, became a radical political act.

'Here, did you see Nicola's new hair? It's fuckin beautiful.'

'Beautiful?' one replied. 'Ha, ha, ha. He just said "beautiful". Ha, ha, ha, mate, you're gay.'

Strangely, the chorus of laughter was, for me, a welcome relief. It's never fun to be laughed at when you don't intend to be funny but my pride was not the only ball in play here. The boys' collective laughter, while humiliating, also signalled they were back to being as they had been before I disorientated them with a foreign idea. An idea which, while simple to me, seemed to threaten them in some way. Instances such as this would happen frequently and produce different results: sometimes you'd get kudos for appearing smart or witty or for dispatching an adversary's attempt to belittle you by retorting with a devastating one-liner. Or you could end up in a heated confrontation simply because an unsanctioned word or reference sparked an escalating tit-for-tat that nobody could back down from without inviting more aggression. In this kind of community people can turn extremely hostile – and dangerous – if they feel put down or threatened.

Was it the word 'beautiful' itself, or what the word 'beautiful' might have implied that created the tension? Perhaps it was the expectation they felt the word placed on them? An expectation to respond in some way and pressure at not knowing how to, or fear of giving a response which was socially unacceptable? An expectation to either disagree or concur and what either response may have revealed about them? What if an accidental smirk or involuntary nod betrayed some secret passion, goofy eccentricity or deep vulnerability they weren't comfortable with other people knowing about? I can only speculate. All I remember is that Nicola's hair was so beautiful I couldn't stop myself saying as much, irrespective of the grief I'd receive. Then again, with a mother like mine, my emotional threshold for feelings of shock, offence and abuse was already painfully high.

4

Gentlemen of the West

MY MUM LEFT the family home when I was about ten years old. I remember coming home one day to find her standing outside the house with my sister, having been gone for a couple of weeks. They came into the house for a while and I recall an argument between her and my dad. Then she went away with my sister and never came back. It wasn't the first time they had broken up. It's funny how you blame yourself for these things even at this young age. It's probably a mixture of wishful thinking and childlike egotism to think that if only you were somehow better, your parents would be able to work out their differences. From then on, we didn't see my mum with any reliability. When we did, the quality of our time with her was patchy. This was mainly due to her drunkenness or preoccupation with obtaining booze. But things quickly brush over you at this age, either because you are too aloof or because it makes it easier to cope. I remember a brief honeymoon period after she left when life felt much more peaceful. My relationship with my little brother, thanks to football and wrestling, really began to blossom. It wasn't until I started attending secondary school a few years later that I began to feel the impact of the abandonment. It led to a deep insecurity.

This manifested itself in many ways and, at its worst, was physically unbearable to experience. It began with fear that people did not like me or that I was in imminent danger. I also longed for a connection, because it seemed to soothe the symptoms of the insecurity, and I would form deep emotional attachments to people – especially girls – who paid me the slightest bit of attention. But because I was so used to being let down and rejected by my mother, I was always on high alert that the people I felt attached to were going to hurt, betray or leave me. Abandonment was such a strong theme at this point in my life that I actively sought this pattern out in all my relationships, without even realising it, and began to confuse deep feelings of emotional insecurity with being in love.

These niggling psychological difficulties, coupled with the generally aggressive social environment, made it hard for me to concentrate on schoolwork. My head was always racing with internal dialogue about the various fears and anxieties I had. I was always rehearsing conversations I might have or replaying old ones over again. It seemed fear was the only thing capable of concentrating my mind. This made learning difficult, especially when it came to subjects I struggled with. Another thing that made this school such a challenging place to learn was that so many other pupils had similar problems.

Crookston Castle Secondary School was built in the early 1950s. It was designed to be repurposed into a military hospital, should the need arise. Back then, at the dawn of the Cold War, who'd have thought it would be the school itself that turned into a war zone? The school took its name from the medieval castle grounds in which it was set. Crookston Castle stood 500 yards from the edge of the playground, encircled by a deep moat at the highest point in Pollok. However, despite being a very well preserved historical monument, nobody seemed to go there very much. I always felt this was a shame because the summit offered a stunning panoramic view of the area which, despite its glaring flaws, was quite a sight to behold – provided, of course, that it was viewed from a safe enough distance.

Right in the centre of Pollok stood a modest shopping precinct, opened in 1979, called the Pollok Centre. It was about half a mile in length and home to a variety of high street stores and supermarket chains. The centrepiece of the Pollok Centre was a large cuckoo clock, which transfixed successive generations of children with a display of music and robotics every quarter of an hour. Beneath the clock, there was a seating area for people to catch their breath, have something to eat or smoke.

The Pollok Centre stood about half a mile from another place of interest, on the outskirts of the scheme called Pollok Park. This was a sprawling country pile, gifted to the people of Glasgow by the Maxwell family in the early 20th century. From the top of the castle, it was evident that the area had, essentially, been carved out of the countryside. Over the decades, the urban areas of Glasgow expanded and joined up, but Pollok existed on the edge of this and was still very much connected to its more rural past – at least aesthetically. Despite having lots of trees, football fields and leisure spaces, the disparity in the quality of housing on either side of the river was obvious: one side was far more run-down than the other. But this was not, as you might assume, a mark of class, but rather, luck of the draw in terms of what sort of home you were given by the council. New homes were always being built and old ones were always being modernised while other parts were being 'regenerated'.

Most of the people living in Pollok had a council house but this didn't stop us from acting like we had more money than we did. I suspect the deep sense of shame many of us felt about our poverty – and an overwhelming desire to conceal it – was why the Pollok Centre was so popular. Here you could acquire everything you needed to appear better off than you really were: new trainers, tracksuits, chains, rings, football strips and boots. Such sought-after items and accessories were expensive but the price of looking poor was always far higher. Catalogues, like Littlewoods and Kay's, and Provident agents or 'provy-men' (money lenders) came to the rescue of many a single parent throughout the course of the school term. Then there was always the shifty looking guy on the corner who had a few bob – as long as you paid him back on time.

There were pockets of affluence, but they existed in 'outposts' which usually adopted (or retained) a different name. In Pollok, for example, there is an area called 'Old Pollok' which is closer to Pollok Park and is a noticeably nicer place to live. People aren't shy to remind you of the difference and make a social distinction between themselves and the area regarded as 'deprived'.

To the south of the river stood a long line of flat-roofed tenements, encased in grey, roughcast concrete, complete with blue verandas which doubled up as viewing platforms, clothes-horses and ashtrays. You won't be surprised to learn that dampness was an issue in the houses with flat roofs; rainfall, instead of trickling down a slope to a drainage system, would often just linger on the horizontal surface until it found a way into people's homes. On the other side of the river, things appeared far less cluttered. There were wide open spaces, football fields, forests, parks and boulevards punctuated by neatly organised semi-detached, four-in-a-block housing which, when viewed from the castle top, seemed to coil up the hill like the swirl of an ice-cream cone.

From this vantage point you could see the different phases of development that had taken place; some ongoing, some complete and others abandoned as the area continued to expand to meet the demands of population growth. But with every shiny new-build thrown up there was always some other structure falling down – often with people still living in it. It gave Pollok a messy air of incompletion. It felt like a prototype of a real area and it was therefore hard to take much pride in it. Any efforts to keep the place clean and tidy were futile and it was more common to throw litter in the street than put it in a bin. Not many things around here were built to last and broad swathes of housing stock were already earmarked for demolition despite being relatively young in architectural terms. However, my school was an exception to this rule and seemed determined to outlive everything in its vicinity – including many of the children who attended it.

The school sat on the south bank of the Levern, which was less of a river and more a stream of consciousness that carried polythene bags to the Clyde – a real river. We just called it the 'burn'. For us, its main function was to provide a clear territorial faultline over which running gang fights could take place. For generations, groups of young men – and sometimes women – gathered on either side of the various bridges laid down along the burn and provoked each other until a fight broke out. This was a tradition stretching back to the seventies. Most of the time it was harmless; people shouting insults or drunken threats, chasing each other before retreating to their own side. But sometimes it got serious and people got hurt. Other times they got killed.

School forced many of these violent tribal factions under one roof, along with the rest of us, for 35 hours a week. On a grey day, it looked more like a prison facility or a factory, complete with a jagged steel fence stalking the hilly perimeter. It was one of those trend-ridden designs that seem so futuristic and fashionable in their day. The school, like the tenements listed for demolition across the road, had a flat roof. It was so ugly that it became something we not only laughed about, but took a certain pride in. We regarded everything around us as either derelict, dirty or falling into a state of disrepair. Sometimes that was unfair and inaccurate but these tropes about the place being a 'shite-hole' 'fulla junkies' were invoked so regularly that their veracity was irrelevant.

I started secondary in 1996, the year Danny Boyle's film adaptation of Irvine Welsh's *Trainspotting* was released. In four years, I didn't venture too far from Pollok as it was a bit of a stoat into the city centre – around 40 minutes by bus – which was something politicians hoped to remedy by green-lighting a new motorway, much to the anger of many locals. Near the end of my school career, I was venturing beyond the borders of Pollok and across the Clyde to the fabled, almost mythical, West End, where I attended a weekly session with a child psychologist. The appointment was something to look forward to and, apart from breaking up the monotony of a regular school day, it also gave me a couple of hours off the leash to explore the city unsupervised. At lunchtime on Thursday I would leave school and take a short bus trip to Govan before jumping the Underground to Hillhead.

The first thing I remember upon stepping off the escalator and onto the busy street was an odd feeling of relaxation. People here looked and sounded different in a way that was immediately apparent. Where I grew up it was unusual to see people of colour, unless they were behind a shop counter, but here it was very multi-cultural, like the world described in my modern studies class. Where I grew up it was unusual to see clean pavements, but here the streets were in pristine condition and nothing like the turd gauntlet I was accustomed to running every day. Here dogs were attached to leads and walked by their owners, as opposed to the collarless, feral hounds running around outside the shopfront along the road from my house.

Having taken a few moments to catch my breath, adjusting my eyes to the world in wonderful technicolour, I remember my first thought being, 'So, this is how people dress when they aren't afraid of being stabbed?'

The Notre Dame Centre, where I attended my counselling, was five minutes from the affluent strip of town, known as Byres Road. You know when you and your friends attempt to impersonate a stereotypically 'posh' person? Well, the people on Byres Road are what that impersonation is based on. On Byres Road it is not unusual to find a small, fashionable dog waiting in the retro wicker basket of an up-cycled penny-farthing while its owner proceeds into a cafe to politely complain to a barista named Felix about being undercharged for artisan sausage. Byres Road is where I learned that there was more than one type of coffee and that you could drink it in a glass. It's where I discovered that fruit was a pleasure in its own right and not merely a cheap alternative to Haribo. But more importantly, this part of the city was where I was first confronted by the strange idea that living in fear of violence was not, as I had been led to believe, an immaculate fact. Bizarre as this place seemed to me, I was also captivated by it because I would never have thought such an easygoing place could exist – especially in Glasgow. Ironic that I only found myself in this serene part of town because I had to attend anger management.

Using the only thing culturally familiar to me as a means of navigation (the famous Greggs bakery chain), I waded deeper into this unknown territory. Though not before purchasing an obligatory sausage roll, bottle of Coke and a fudge doughnut. Then, up the leafy road I went, feeling very pleased with myself as I charged past local kids nibbling on rabbit food.

Despite this being a densely populated residential area, mature trees flanked slanted tenement flats, leering clumsily over the pavements like lanky security guards. This wasn't the first time I had seen tenement housing of this type but never had I witnessed it in such a grand scale. It was the attention to detail that distinguished the buildings here. It seemed like things gained more value the older they got, as opposed to falling into dereliction. Here things were built to last and the architecture seemed to project that quality outwards. The planners had not foreseen a time when every family here would own at least two cars, but this cramped feeling, rather than a source of stress, merely accentuated the exclusivity and prestige of the area and, by extension, the social status of all therein.

The oddest thing, however, was that you never saw anybody coming or going from those tenements and you never saw neighbours talking to each other. It was almost as if people never grew up here, but instead bought their way in and that their houses were all lying empty because everyone was out at work.

Mind-boggling.

As I continued upwards to the Notre Dame Centre, children from a local school were walking down towards me, on the other side of the road. I immediately sensed they were non-threatening and as they drew closer I overheard them talking. I couldn't quite follow the thread but I could hear enough to know they were using the kind of words that I always had in my head but felt too inhibited to speak. They were expressive and uninhibited with one another. A part of me wanted so much to walk over and join the conversation, as it seemed like we would probably have had a lot of things in common, but as I passed them they suddenly went quiet. Instantly I knew why: that's what you did when you were walking past something that made you anxious.

Falling silent, and perhaps a head bow, was a way of showing deference to a potential threat; a signal you weren't looking for trouble and wished to pass without incident. So often I had executed this exact manoeuvre on my own turf to avoid confrontation. The signal was always a gamble because, once a potential attacker knew for certain that you didn't want to fight, they often took it as a green light to get more aggressive. In this inversion of my usual experience, these kids seemed to perceive me as the threat. It was a jarring role reversal and I experienced a mix of pride at being feared and resentment at feeling misunderstood as I continued up the hill, short of breath, to my destination.

As I approached the building, I replayed the collision of our worlds in my head, imagining alternative scenarios in which I gave the perfect account of myself, before sauntering on, casting a lifelong shadow in the memories of my foolish detractors. An intoxicating bravado took hold as I agonised about why the group fell silent as they passed me. I reasoned that I had been harshly judged by snobs who could do with a clip around the ears as an introduction to the 'real world'. A real world where I lived and of which they knew little. And then the vengeful thought occurred to me that should I ever be confronted by this flock of straight-laced mummy's boys again, I would not hesitate to call them all gay.

5

The Trial

INCIDENTS LIKE THAT, where I would attempt to mix with people from a higher social class but come away feeling harshly judged, were very rare in my childhood. But as I got older, and able to leave Pollok occasionally, these awkward interactions became more frequent. As inconsequential as they were, when taken in isolation, they eventually culminated in a belief that would reframe my view of the world for years to come. Those botched attempts to move among the affluent became the germinal events that eventually led to my deep sense of grievance with anyone I perceived as well-off. In my community some people fought about football, others over politics and religion. But my simmering resentment, if not concentrated completely on my mother, lay with those in society who appeared to be doing much better than the rest of us, those who were gliding through life unimpeded by the constraints of poverty and the material disadvantage and self-doubt that comes with it.

I say that as if one day I just woke up, ready for a revolution, having become a class warrior overnight. Maybe I'd like to think so, but that was not the case. The truth is, it was a gradual process where my personal experience and the class politics of my community, in which I was steeped, converged in my late teens. While I may have been too young to truly comprehend the complexity of the issues at play, what I did get was that everyone I had grown up with was really pissed off and that I should be too. In fact, it was almost rude – taboo even – not to be angry at something and so long as your anger was directed at one of the many sanctioned targets, then there would be no shortage of allies to validate your grievance. This feeling of justifiable anger at the state of things, whether it be my community or even my own life, always led to some form of blame being ascribed to another group in society and, for me, middle class people fitted the bill perfectly. This bee in my bonnet has been a constant and finds expression as a sense of irritation at certain people I assume are posh; I can be irritated by an opinion, an accent, an accessory or an item of clothing. I suspect the thing I'm really annoyed at is what I perceive as their relative prosperity and privilege and this, in turn, makes everything else about them suspect and annoying. My tendency towards class stereotyping can be triggered at any time but was stirred by something terrible last April. My relapse into class stereotyping happened, as it often does, by turning on a British television and watching whatever appears for more than a few minutes.

The news agenda was dominated by one story: the plight of a suburban couple who were challenging a court decision to uphold a fine for taking their child on holiday during the school term. The local authority had advised the family that taking their daughter on a foreign trip would be in breach of the rules. But the rascals decided to go anyway. When the fine was issued, David Platt contested it and eventually the dispute ended up in the courts. Interesting enough, if not a little twee. It wasn't so much the story that bothered me but the disproportionate amount of coverage it received, presented in print, online and on television as a David and Goliath tale of one intrepid father's fight against a tyrannical nanny state attempting to dictate how he should raise his own child.

The editor of the *Sunday Times* even appeared on BBC *News* arguing passionately, for over five minutes, that a sensible application of the law was required in this instance. By sensible, she meant that the law should be carefully interpreted and enforced in such a way as to account for the nuance and complexities of each case – as opposed to a blanket, one-size-fits-all approach.

I almost spat my coffee out laughing.

This, after all, is the primary complaint of anyone who has ever been convicted of a crime. People who are convicted of crimes very rarely think the law has been applied fairly to them. This is as true of serial killers as it is of petty thieves. Most people find it hard to accept even the most banal forms of legal responsibility. Think how indignant drivers get when they receive legitimate parking tickets or speeding fines. Everyone always has a good reason as to why they are the exception to a rule they are being subjected to and it's very rare that a person holds their hands up and accepts culpability. Most people believe their circumstances are unique and that the rules shouldn't apply. The difference between most people who go through the court system and the Platt family is, arguably, a matter of class.

Now can I just say that before proceeding with an argument about class, it's sometimes considered very rude not to define what is meant by 'middle class'. Some 'middle class' people – despite being 'middle class' – don't regard themselves as 'middle class', so they find it offensive when you call them 'middle class'. They require a definition, not because they are especially interested in accuracy or specifics, but so that they can exclude themselves from whatever type of 'middle class' people they think you're going to criticise. I just want you all to know, from the outset, that I am sensitive to these needs. In this book, we will be using the Stewart Lee definition.

Lee's comedy, for more than 20 years, has worked precisely because his audience tacitly accept his on-stage persona as being middle class. As far as I am aware, nobody has interrupted his show to demand that he first defines what he means by 'middle class' before proceeding with this act. And there's a reason for that: Stewart Lee is middle class so people just take his word for it. Someone like me, on the other hand, must submit a definition for review before setting forth an opinion. Well, not in this book. So, how can I be so sure the Platts, fined for insisting on taking their daughter out of school during the school term, are middle class or affluent? Well, I can't. But there are a few indicators they are. The first indicator is the direct involvement of the *Sunday Times*. The *Sunday Times* didn't just cover the story but appeared to become advocates of the couple. At the risk of seeming cynical, this was likely because this story, about middle class people, was of interest to their readers, who are middle class. Then again, perhaps I'm taking another leap here. In that case, let's establish who reads the *Sunday Times* and what they might tell us about the social status of the Platts.

Sunday Times readers fall into the ABC1 demographic. In UK news media, ABC1 is one of several ways the industry categorises its audience. Funnily enough, it's a class-based analysis and one so brazen, Karl Marx himself would likely have been offended by it. In the *Cambridge Dictionary*, ABC1 is defined as 'one of the three higher social and economic groups, which consist of people who have more education and better-paid jobs than those in other groups'.

This style of classification was developed by the National Readership Survey, which used social grades, represented by letters and numbers. For many of you in the lower categories, the news you are being classified in this way by your faithful tabloid newspaper may be surprising – and offensive.

Grade	Chief income earner's occupation	Frequency in 2008
A	Higher managerial, administrative or professional	14 per cent
B	Intermediate managerial, administrative or professional	23 per cent
C1	Supervisory or clerical and junior managerial, administrative or professional	29 per cent
C2	Skilled manual workers	21 per cent
D	Semi-skilled and unskilled manual workers	15 per cent
E	Casual or lowest grade workers, pensioners, and others who depend on the welfare state for their income	8 per cent

Source: Wikipedia

People in the lower classification are regarded as culturally unsophisticated and parochial in their concerns. That's why there are lots of big colour pictures in the papers you read and why stories and features are written with an assumption that you don't know big words like 'bloviating' and 'verbosely'. It's not that the journalists and editors think you're stupid. It's just that they think you're stupid enough that you won't notice you're reading the news equivalent of a kid's menu. They don't think you're daft, they just assume you are too preoccupied with everything that being lower class entails to think beyond your next Crispy Pancake.

I'm often being told we live in a classless society. If that's the case then somebody better tell the media that class isn't a real thing anymore, because I don't think they've got the news yet. As evidenced by the table, ABC1 means upper middle class, middle class and lower middle class. When a newspaper like the *Sunday Times* comes to your aid then there's a slight chance it's because, like their readership, you are part of that middle class demographic.

Still not convinced? Still think I'm jumping to conclusions? Okay, well what about the minor detail of the Platts' contested holiday being in Florida, which as I'm sure you're aware is a renowned global hot spot for the world's poor. This is an area of America that is so politically enfranchised, presidencies are often won and lost based on the oscillating whims of a few thousand perma-tanned rollerbladers. Flights alone, to a destination like Florida, cost more than most all-inclusive holidays to Europe for an average family of four. But who knows, maybe the Platts had been saving stamps at the Co-op for 45 years or recently had taken out a Wonga loan? Who am I to cast such wild aspersions? So, what other evidence is there to support my proposition that they are 'middle class'?

Okay, well how about we eliminate the possibility they are working class then? The first red flag the Platts are not working class is the fact Jon 'I know better than the courts' Platt used the word 'unfettered' when describing the discretion teachers exercise over the rules around attendance. A working class person wouldn't risk saying something so gay in public. Second, this whole episode started because Jon 'this is about principle' Platt refused to pay a £60 fine. What sort of person would voluntarily put themselves in court for such a paltry sum of money? A working class person would have ignored the letter or agreed to pay the fine down in weekly instalments.

Next, the Platts live in the Isle of Wight. While I'm sure not everybody who lives there is well-off, it's evident quite a few folks are doing reasonably well, financially at least. 41 per cent of households own their home outright. A further 29 per cent own with a mortgage. In short, 70 per cent of households are owned compared to 68 per cent for southeast England – the UK's most prosperous region. There are more homeowners where Jon 'it's a shame for us' Platt lives than there are in the poshest part of the country.

The next indicator Jon 'victim of the system' Platt is a little too smart to be a C2DE tabloid reading, hard-hat wearing, building site dwelling, portaloo shitting, Betfred dreaming, nose-picking pleb is the fact he not only holidays in Florida, says words like unfettered out loud and lives in one of the most affluent areas of Britain, but Jon 'I'm doing this for the people' Platt also runs a PPI claims firm. PPI firms are the bane of working class people's evenings the country over. PPI claims firms are, predatory businesses that cold-call financially illiterate people to alert them they've been conned by a bank. The firms then offer to fill out some forms on their behalf and post them to a bank – in exchange for thousands of pounds. If you're still not convinced then what about the fact Jon 'tear down the nanny state' Platt, still managed to claim legal aid – even though he voluntarily brought the case to court? Yes, that's right, Mr Platt knowingly broke the rules and then voluntarily took the case to court – and you paid for it. If Jon Platt had a brass neck, it'd be worth millions.

By now I think you're getting a real sense of this class-based irritation I described earlier, and what it does to me. I'm sure you also have an outgroup that provokes similarly strong and irrational reactions in you. Maybe it's people like me, engaging in blatant reverse snobbery, that really get on your tits? And like me, I'm sure you have an armoury of justifications that explain why your own brand of hypocrisy is legitimate. So here's one of mine:

What escaped many people's notice, as they squandered

attention on Jon 'but kids learn more from a holiday in Florida than they do in school' Platt, was that new rules about tax credits came into effect that very same day. Child tax credit is a state benefit in the United Kingdom made available to people in low income employment. The benefit tops up wages and is paid out to people with children. But since the economic crash of 2008, in an age of permanent austerity, many benefits have been cut, tightened or withdrawn to bring down the 'deficit'. The same day the Platts were all over the news, a cap came into effect meaning people could only claim tax credits for two children at the most. That's contentious enough but it wasn't the whole story. We also learned of circumstances where exemptions could apply, meaning the benefit could be paid for more than two children in some cases. One exemption, now known widely as the 'rape' clause, allows a woman to claim for more than two children if the additional child was conceived by sexual assault. Yes, that's correct, women would be permitted to claim in-work benefit for a third child but with the caveat that their father must be a rapist.

It's one of those difficult areas of public policy, where a line must be drawn and the line inadvertently reveals our moral confusion as a society.

Oddly, however, the media was a bit less interested in this. It simply wasn't riveting or glamorous enough. Either that, or it just didn't hit their radar. Perhaps it was because so many people in media fall into the ABC1 demographic and are less likely to be affected by changes to benefits. But can you imagine the furore in newsrooms up and down the country, had an affluent and socially respectable couple, like the Platts, been forced to endure the same kind of indignity? I mean, if a self-imposed £60 fine was enough to mobilise the entire UK press to their cause – even though they voluntarily broke the rules – then imagine the outrage something akin to a rape clause would provoke if it was going to affect the unimpeachable ABC1 demographic? The big difference between the Platts and the women subject to the rape clause, or people on benefits generally, is that one group is more likely to speak up. Not only speak up, but more likely to possess the knowledge, resources and agency to make their voice heard and, crucially, for that voice to be taken seriously. The court system is full of people being hit with fines, disposal orders and custodial sentences every single day but only a select number of cases receive prominence in the news. Even fewer receive generous coverage.

Now let me say that I'm aware some may disagree that these two cases are connected. Some may even think it vulgar that I have chosen to contrast them in this way. But equivalences like this are precisely how many of us arrive at our opinions. What I've just done is what people generally do when they turn on the news; observing complicated matters from a distance, we rush to conclusions about the nature of society and our place within it. These conclusions become the basis of new beliefs whether they are true or false. Every day we turn on our televisions or pick up our newspapers and we make the exact same sort of leap I just made here: we decide that some other group is always being privileged above our own. That this group benefits from a slew of unseen advantages we can't quite put our finger on but are certain they exist. We feel like the people who make the news – and the rules – are either too removed from the reality of our lives to accurately portray them, or worse, that they are deliberately misrepresenting us as part of some broader conspiracy. We draw conclusions about why and how this happens and these conclusions become the windows through which we see the world.

Sometimes we're wrong, sometimes we aren't. But what if the conclusions you drew led to a belief that there was no point in participating at all? What if you decided that the political process, at every level, was designed to exclude you? Political apathy is a trait often associated with the lower classes but we rarely examine why. If we ever do examine it, we blame the poor for being disinterested or narrowminded. Apathy in many communities might have something to do with people drawing equivalences like I just did, from a cascade of news that appears to suggest different rules apply to different types of people. On the day women were legally obliged to provide proof of their rape to claim benefit designed to ease the burden of in-work poverty on their children, the national news was dominated by a family who felt hard done by because they were fined £60 for taking their daughter to Florida. I'm not saying both parties do not have the right to feel equally aggrieved at their respective circumstances, but surely one deserves more prominence than the other in the public mind?

This is the other 'deficit' we rarely talk about or acknowledge. The deficit in our respective experiences when we come from lower class or higher class backgrounds. The deficit in how that experience is represented, reported and discussed. This deficit, which appears to be widening, has led to a culture that leaves many people feeling excluded, isolated or misrepresented and, therefore, adversarial or apathetic towards it. And it's often based on people living in run-down social conditions, with little money, in stressed-out, violent communities, turning on the television and making observations like the one I just made about the Platts. It's the belief that the system is rigged against you and that all attempts to resist or challenge it are futile. That the decisions that affect your life are being taken by a bunch of other people somewhere else who are deliberately trying to conceal things from you. A belief that you are excluded from taking part in the conversation about your own life. This belief is deeply held by people in many communities and there is a very good reason for it: it's true.

6

No Mean City

NEWS AND CULTURE, generally, are two domains where we can see clearly how social inequality expresses itself. Another realm where this deficit in our experience of society can be found is in the respective living standards of the social classes. This is not to say that everyone is entitled to equally high quality housing or that all social housing is inferior to all private housing. It's simply acknowledging another area where we can see a clear gulf between the haves and have-nots. These gulfs are important to acknowledge wherever they are found, because they may explain why people from certain social backgrounds often think, feel and behave differently. Understanding how things like living conditions impact our respective long term attitudes and outcomes in life is key to grappling with the finer points of social inequality. Finer points that are often contested because they get lost in translation when we try to communicate across the widening ravine of class divides.

You don't have to be a professor of architecture to notice the historic gulf between the classes when it comes to housing quality; in Glasgow, high-rise social housing is synonymous with deprivation. Like many of the stereotypes surrounding deprived communities, the notion that high-rises are unpleasant places to live is not untrue but is slightly unfair: many examples of thriving high-rise communities exist and not all tower blocks are dangerous, drug-ridden, or crime-infested. Even the monstrosities that gave rise to the gritty stereotype weren't all bad. But enough of them were – or still are – bad enough that their reputation, fair or not, precedes them.

Like many hapless eras of human endeavour, it's easy to look back in hindsight and sneer at those who naively approved a building programme that would come to symbolise urban decay and social dereliction: the idea of stacking poor people vertically, which probably seemed rather clever in the mid-20th century, when decades of population growth, fuelled by consecutive industrial revolutions, was the curtain raiser to a new rotating cast of social problems that would characterise poverty for decades to come.

In the grip of economic expansion at the end of the 19th century, with so many material spoils to pursue – and plenty of work available – it would have been hard for some to foresee (or care about) the sociocultural blowback lurking on the hazy, smoke-filled horizon as western civilisation bellowed, burned and steamed its way confidently into the 20th century. This period of economic growth led to the creation of the modern world and remains unparalleled in human history. It was the first time living standards and wages had risen consistently and mass production, made possible by manufacturing machinery, wrought changes on industry as well as the emerging global economy. But nowhere was this change more tangible than in the lives of ordinary working people, which were fundamentally transformed by technology.

This phase of growth, fuelled by imperial adventure, over-reached and inevitably slowed. As the British Empire receded from every corner of the globe after the First World War, the unforeseen social consequences of such rapid population growth began to find expression, not only in an economic depression, but more ominously, in the social conditions, health and behaviour of the lower classes.

In Glasgow, the Second City of the Empire, successful industrial suburbs like the Gorbals, where native and immigrant populations had exploded in the 19th century, became culturally strained, diseased and unliveable. Workers, growing tired of the poor living standards and atrocious working conditions, began to organise and forced concessions from government that became the basis of human rights in areas like employment and housing. These included a reduction in the working week as well as the first

Housing Act, in 1919, guaranteeing the basic living standards we now take for granted like electricity, running water and flushing toilets.

Despite these advances, by the 1930s the descent of the Gorbals into deprivation continued and the area soon became a byword for violence: often referred to as the most dangerous place in the UK. Britain's social housing stock had been hastily fashioned to meet rising demand and, in Glasgow, it wasn't long before the homes, then providing accommodation to roughly 500,000 people, became untenable. Families of five, six and more were often crammed into single rooms on street after street of run-down tenement housing.

A range of solutions were proposed. One involved the design and creation of 'housing schemes': residential areas built on the city's outer rim that made use of wide-open space away from the inner city. These would help to ease the burden on areas like the Gorbals, which were now dangerously overcrowded. These housing schemes would utilise the extra space and, as well as rehousing families in modern accommodation, would also provide leisure space. However, these plans were interrupted by the Second World War and not resumed for many years. The government's 'after war' programme pledged to build 50,000 new homes per year in a bid to clear the slums. But unlike the housing schemes like Pollok, Easterhouse and Castlemilk, which lay on the outskirts of Glasgow, back in the city, ground space was scarce and this presented a challenge for planners.

In the '50s, high-rise social housing, imported from continental Europe, was touted as the solution for these inner city urban areas and by the '60s, high-flying architects like Sir Basil Spence were parachuted in to redesign the slums. 'When you're crammed for space', said one news reporter, 'you have to build high', the footage appearing in the 1993 documentary *High Rise and Fall*. As the film vividly illustrates, build high is exactly what they did. Iconic multi-storey structures rose from the ashes of the slums, a fitting tribute to the skyward ambitions of the city's people. But, while the housing schemes appeared, at least initially, to be a success, to the horror of politicians and residents alike, within 18 months locals had renamed the Queen Elizabeth tower blocks Alcatraz, Barlinnie and Carstairs – two being violent prisons and the other a Scottish hospital for the criminally insane.

Many of the tower blocks, despite their early promise, came to be regarded by locals as dirty, dangerous and undesirable places to live. As well as structural problems that created dampness, and windows that were known for blowing in during high winds, drug dealers lurked on the periphery, looking for new economic opportunities to exploit. As traditional industries like steel and coal were wound down, unemployment rose and many people became idle and demoralised. The undeniable failure of tower block housing in this part of the city – and others like it – was devastating, not only for local officials but more so for residents, who had just moved out of slums to start their new lives in the 'skyscrapers' of the future.

These multi-storey 'gardens in the sky' and the socialist principles they embodied were not only grand but also earnest and ambitious attempts to substantially raise the standard of living for working class people; going as far as integrating the rich and storied history of the local community into the contours of the architecture itself. Spence, designer of the infamous Queen Elizabeth high-rises that became the ground zero of the horrendous stereotype, envisioned that the three towers, side-by-side, would give the majestic appearance of tall ships in full sail.

It's a lovely idea, but as one resident, referring to the maritime motif, observed: 'The only way you got that impression was if you walked over to Richmond Park' – a green space easily a mile from the tower blocks. It's quite absurd to think that this potentially awe-inspiring tribute to European utopianism, which seamlessly consummated the union of high art and social need, only cohered when viewed from a distance. A far less pretentious way of saying this is simply that the flats made more sense the further away from them you got – which created a dilemma for the people living there. There was something about the way Spence perceived the community that was fatally flawed. Something about the assumptions he made about what working class people wanted and needed that no amount of technical skill, artistic flair or noble intentions could correct. A lack of consultation with the community itself, about their needs and aspirations, and a design phase riddled with well-meaning but privileged assumptions, meant that within 20 years many of these cutting-edge structures were either being torn down, scheduled for demolition or superficially modified to give a less brutal appearance. And in communities like the Gorbals, gathering excitedly to watch their history being razed to the ground has not only become a tradition, but an expectation. One which endures to this very day.

High-rise housing in the Gorbals was a humbling and costly lesson in urban regeneration and the cultural legacy for these missteps still casts a long shadow on the city. Thousands of families, already struggling to make ends meet, were placed under so much strain that it altered them physically, psychologically and emotionally. What was left of the local economy adapted to supply the community's mutating demands; off licences, pubs, chip shops, licensed bingo halls, bookmakers and, latterly, drug dealers, provided temporary relief from the grim reality of deindustrialisation. But these seemingly harmless activities soon became vices that would later find expression as public health epidemics. In such oppressive and downtrodden social conditions, people began to distrust public institutions and the various authority figures, like police and social workers, despatched to mop up the rising tide of social problems.

Meanwhile, in the more troubled pockets of these challenged communities, people hid themselves away in a dark underbelly and attempted to raise children while descending into sordid lives of alcoholism and substance misuse.

One of those children was called Sandra Gallagher. My mother.

7

Nineteen Eighty-four

MY MUM AND dad met at a rehearsal studio in Glasgow in the summer of 1983. My dad, 19 years old, was an aspiring musician with hopes of getting signed to a record label. One evening, after a practice, another band member's girlfriend showed up with one of her pals. My dad and she hit it off. Not long after, they decided to go camping together on the Isle of Arran. Before their weekend of teenage love was over, they ran out of money and had to abandon the campsite without paying. In some ways, it is quite a romantic story, in others, an ominous sign of things to come.

Not long after they were back on the mainland, my mum took my dad to meet her family in the Gorbals. The night began as you would expect; a warm welcome, friendly banter and food and drink aplenty. But tension began to fill the air as the booze started to flow, and it wasn't long until a fight broke out between my mother and her mother. My dad, who was also living in an alcoholic home in Pollok, was accustomed to the tropes of a wet household. But something about my mum's family was different. There was an extra element of unpredictability and danger at play here. The boundaries of what was and wasn't appropriate were not as well defined. Before the night was through, a massive fight erupted. It was so bad that, on that night, my dad decided he was going to end the relationship with my mother.

But, on the day he decided to tell her it was over, she revealed she was pregnant. The following April, I was born. They called me Darren because 'Arran' was, apparently, a bit too 'American sounding'. My mother lived with us until I was about ten. During that decade, she left a life-altering trail of carnage in her wake; each year her behaviour was more bizarre and unpredictable than the next.

One sunny afternoon in Pollok, not long before she left, I arrived with a couple of friends in tow, to find many of the contents of our home laid out in the front garden, incinerated.

I can't recall what explanation I offered my friends, though I suspect none was required. They already had some insight into how we lived. When you live in a troubled home, life spills out onto the street. Eventually you become closed off to the dysfunction, perhaps to spare yourself feelings of shame or embarrassment. You adjust to the fact that people in the community know your business and are probably judging you. Privacy becomes another elusive luxury beyond the reach of people like you.

Dignity was for the fancy people.

Pretending you're not poor is one thing. All you need to pull that off is a couple of credit cards, a catalogue and a deep delusional streak. It also helps your street credibility if you keep that big blue crate of European Union stew that you've received for free as a poverty perk well out of view if you have visitors round. But concealing family dysfunction is much trickier. For one, the dysfunction may be out of your control; a parent or sibling, for example. Second, the dysfunction may be imperceptible to you and therefore hard to hide. Dysfunction, like poverty, can lead to disfigurements which are visible to everyone but you. Turns out, when you are living in dysfunction, it doesn't occur to you that this is the case.

By the time it becomes apparent that your life isn't normal, it's too late to keep up the pretence. Concerned neighbours hear your troubles through the walls. Teachers, doctors, social workers and mental health professionals are aware of your ongoing situation. But for every person showing concern or offering support, there's another waiting to exploit the vulnerability. Just like the inmates in the prison cafeteria who'll slash each other over toast, if only to stave off more violence further down the line, I was forced either to confront or submit to the predators in my midst; the dysfunction at home, mainly around my mother, as well as the obvious fact we were poor, was something I had to account for when I was at school. On a few occasions I arrived there after dressing myself and became the butt of playground teasing. One morning, I remember my dad having to leave work to come to the school with a proper outfit for me. God knows what I was wearing. There were other occasions when I'd be sitting at the reception of nursery or school, well after the end of the school day, waiting for someone to come and pick me up.

I remember climbing onto a kitchen worktop to gain access to a cupboard so that I could make my breakfast; but, too young to know how to do it, pouring cold water into a bowl of oats and eating it before getting myself ready for school. At the time, this was no big deal. I was already adapting to the fact my mother was not fit to take care of me. The only problem was that while this all seemed perfectly normal to me, having nothing else to compare it to, it was obvious to other people, not least merciless kids, that something wasn't right.

Thankfully, God gave me a full head of ginger hair and a pale, freckle-dotted face, guaranteeing me safe passage through the playground every day without much incident. Difficult as school could be, I always found it preferable to the unpredictability of life at home, where I would spend a lot of time walking on eggshells, ascertaining what sort of mood my mother was in.

On a few occasions, I'd run out to the back garden and throw her empty bottles over the spiky steel fence. If I recall correctly, this was pitched to me like a game. No doubt I knew exactly what it was, but played along to amuse her. Much like the time I spent in the amusements, having been promised a day in 'Treasure Island', only to spend the afternoon amusing myself in a toy car, staring at the 'insert credit' screen, while she plunged the family silver manically into a slot machine. Days like that, or chucking bottles over the back fence for her, were about as close to quality time as we ever got. Years later, I went through the fence to explore the woods behind the house and was shocked at the number of bottles that had been thrown over. The eight foot high fence, spanning the length of our street, had recently been erected to deter housebreakers. They wouldn't have gotten much had they been daft enough to break into our gaff, given that my mum had sold or pawned whatever valuable possessions we had. She even started borrowing money from our neighbours when my dad was at work. Her drink and drug problem was so out of control it was severely impairing her ability to care for us, placing us in immediate danger. It wasn't long before syringes appeared in the garden.

One afternoon, I managed to climb out of my first-floor bedroom window and perch myself on the window sill above the concrete slabs, oblivious to the fact that, had I fallen, I might have been killed; to me, this was just another adventure until I was rudely interrupted by a neighbour screaming at the top of her lungs, 'Darren McGarvey, get in, right now!' This was not the first time I had been involved in a window-related incident. A couple of years before, in our second family flat, I had somehow managed to push a cat out of a window from the top floor of a three-storey tenement. For some reason, when animals came to harm it seemed to upset my mother far more than when I did. She was crying as she ran down the stairs. The cat was later put down. She seemed less bothered by my proximity to an open window than about the family pet, perhaps a symptom of her bizarre priorities.

It was in this flat that her heavy drinking first became apparent to my dad. Having been trusted with his cheque book to pay the mortgage, she started cashing generous cheques to purchase alcohol and drugs. We had to give up that flat and move back to Pollok, and into council housing, as my mum had effectively bankrupted us and defaulted on the mortgage. We didn't last long in the next house either, this being our third in as many years. My dad continued to work and provide, and she continued to drink while attempting to conceal it. Not long after the birth of my sister in 1987, my mum bought some heroin with the intention of selling it, but subsequently smoked and injected it all with the help of some friends. She ran up a massive drug debt. Within a few weeks my dad had been attacked outside our home and threatened, that should the debt remain unpaid, we would all be killed. My mum, having temporarily returned to the Gorbals, got wind of this and approached gangsters she knew from her own area, to get the dealers in Pollok off my dad's back. We moved to yet another house on the other side of Pollok, this time during the night. Even so, Dad believed the dealers knew our location and that the reprisal was still imminent. All we could do was get on with our lives. There were days when all he could do was wait. Thankfully, the dealers never came. It seems my mother did have her occasional uses, and had redeemed this desperate situation by getting her 'friends' in the Gorbals to persuade the dealers to write off the debt.

I wouldn't have judged my dad for wanting to be put out of his misery.

8

A Question of Loyalties

UNSURPRISINGLY, WHEN YOU are living in a community where things like this are a regular occurrence, it's hard to be optimistic. In areas like Pollok, there's a higher prevalence of this sort of dysfunction and while it may not directly affect everyone, it does have a corrosive effect on the morale and esteem of the community. When you are always hearing stories about violent incidents taking place, or people complaining of problems local politicians won't do anything about, it adds to the sense that you live in a run-down place that's been largely forgotten by wider society – until something terrible happens and your scheme is front page news.

In poorer communities, there is a pervasive belief that things will never change; that those with power or authority are self-serving and not to be trusted. This may seem like a self-defeating view to take, and in many ways, it is. But if you spend more than a few weeks living in a typically deprived community, you'll soon learn what it's deprived of, because the problems are not difficult to identify. What's difficult is how many walls you come up against when you try to do anything about it. In these communities, the desire to participate is, in many ways, beaten out of people. It's always assumed that poverty is a by-product of apathy; that the poor remain so because they are inactive with respect to the business of their own lives. But often the opposite is true. Enthusiasm to take part and be active in communities quickly dissipates when people realise the local democracy isn't really designed with them in mind; that it's designed primarily so that people from outside the community can retain control of it, over the heads of those who live there.

One of the main ways like-minded people who want to achieve a shared ambition attempt to get active locally is by setting up a group. In working class communities these objectives are pretty straightforward. Usually people just want a space where they can engage in an activity they enjoy or benefit from. But setting up a group isn't as easy as it sounds. If you want to set up a group or an organisation, you first need a 'board'. A board requires at least three people, a written constitution adopted by the board, and a bank account. If you don't have a board you can't access money. If you don't have a constitution you can't open a bank account. If you don't have a bank account you can't access funding to rent premises. And that's just the tip of the iceberg as far as the tortuous local bureaucracy is concerned. Don't get me wrong, you are free to go rogue and form your own group – with no board – if you like, but you won't get a bean towards the running costs. If you do manage to conform to the necessary formal structure required in order to get legally recognised, you then have the funding hoops to jump through.

Money might be made available for groups with certain objectives, but people at community level have no way of influencing how these are set. Essentially, this creates a dynamic where people at grassroots level are corralled into setting up groups that indirectly do the bidding of central government – because it's hard to get supported for doing anything else. Working class folk receive strange looks when asked what their group's lofty objectives are and they respond simply by saying they just want a place to make tea and coffee for the elderly. Or somewhere for teenagers to hang out. Or cooking classes for single parents. Or football or fishing. The things they want are often so straightforward that it's baffling to middle class ears. There is a big disconnect between the grand social engineering agenda of government and the far simpler, unglamorous aspirations and needs of local people, many of whom are not fluent in the ways of jargon.

The system is set up for working class people to be 'engaged' by 'facilitators' and 'mentors', who help them water down whatever they want to do in order that community aspirations align with those in positions of influence or power. The board structure creates a mechanism by which a group can be commandeered at any time should it begin to get a little too above its station. Glasgow poet and essayist Tom Leonard satirises this phenomenon, where the poor are effectively chaperoned around their own lives by the middle class, in 'Liason Co-ordinator'. This poem addresses the issue of class and how it is reinforced through language. The words 'Liason Co-ordinator' alone arouse suspicion. This is the sort of jargon that a certain type of person speaks in. The poem also shows the assumptions commonly made in poorer communities about people on the other side of the class divide, who they often regard as exploitative and patronising. Sometimes that's fair and sometimes it isn't, but bridging these gulfs is the central challenge of our time.

As social inequality widens and the chasms in our relative experiences become more pronounced, we make assumptions about the people on the other side of the divide, their lifestyle and beliefs, their intentions towards us. These projections don't account for the complexity and richness of people's lives. This is what makes talking about class so difficult.

Whichever side of the tracks you come from, it is likely that you harbour unconscious beliefs and attitudes about the issue of class; about yourself and the people across the way. For me it was this idea that middle class people have it easy, are born with a silver spoon in their mouth and benefit from a plethora of unseen advantages that I do not. For you, maybe it's a belief that people stay poor because they don't work hard enough, or that the system is fair and people's negative attitudes that are holding them back. Our beliefs are a bit like lenses that appear to bring the world into clearer focus. The conclusions we draw, based on what we think we are seeing, are extremely important, not only because they become cornerstones of our thinking, but also because there's a link between what we believe and how we subsequently behave. Our beliefs, whether true or false, often extend into the realm of political participation, one of the few areas where people from lower and middle class backgrounds still intersect in any meaningful way.

The problem is, these false beliefs about each other, often based on stereotypes and hyperbole reinforced over generations on either side of the divide, make dialogue in the political domain extremely challenging. Worse still, the fall-out when attempts at dialogue fail becomes the basis of yet more resentment and misunderstanding. In Pollok, this tension between the concerns and culture of working class people and those from more affluent backgrounds, who tended to be in positions of influence or authority, was the crucible of my early political experience. But rather than challenge assumptions about class, these confrontations deepened the divide. And when this tension eventually came to a head, it literally changed the shape and face of our community.

9

On the Road

'THE SAID LANDS should remain forever as open spaces of woodland for the enhancement of the beauty of the neighbourhood and so far, as possible for the benefit of the citizens of Glasgow.' Those were the words of Sir John Maxwell when he bequeathed his estate, known as Pollok Park, to the people of the city in 1939. However, in 1974 the National Trust for Scotland, entrusted with the land, decided to relax the conditions of the previous agreement concerning the park – so that a motorway could be built through it.

Activist and academic, Paul Routledge, in his paper, 'The Imagineering of Resistance: Pollok Free State and the practice of postmodern politics' (which I will channel and paraphrase throughout this chapter), outlines the germinal events that culminated in the campaign to oppose the road:

> Concerted protests against the (M77) motorway began in 1978 and involved Corkerhill Community Council and other concerned community groups.
>
> In 1988, a public inquiry into the motorway issue lasted for three months and included an array of submissions against the M77. This included opposition from Glasgow District Council, local communities who would be affected by the M77 and various community organisations including Glasgow for People. However, despite popular resistance to the motorway, preliminary construction commenced in 1992. A swath was cut through the western side of Pollok estate and the preliminary foundations of the road laid.

Despite local people mobilising to make their voices heard, over a period of nearly 30 years, they were, effectively, ignored. A dizzying array of justifications were given: the motorway would assist economic development, save travelling time for road users, improve the reliability of public transport as well as enhance environmental conditions and reduce road accidents. Opponents of the road disputed these claims and set forth their own case that the M77 would increase noise and air pollution, cause damage to the woodland and wildlife in Pollok estate as well as substantially increase traffic.

They argued that the resources used to construct the M77 would be better directed to upgrading existing transport facilities; and that the motorway would benefit car users from affluent areas as opposed to the local communities, where ownership and use of cars was low. Routledge writes:

> In addition, the construction of the road would sever the access of these local communities to the Pollok estate – a safe recreational area for children – and place a loud, polluting, motorway close to primary and secondary schools. Politically, the construction of the motorway would entail the commercial development of a green belt space and the subsequent restriction of public access to the land.

In response, a band of environmentalists calling themselves the Pollok Free State set up camp in Pollok Country Park, which they claimed was the property of the people. Led by craftsman and environmentalist Colin Macleod, who began a tree top protest against the motorway in the early '90s, the Pollok Free State quickly became a beacon of resistance, community empowerment and democracy.

Its aim was not only to block the unwanted road but also to raise the democratic issue of the rights of local people to have a say over how public space is used and developed. It was part of a bigger 'No M77' protest involving many groups at the time, including Scottish Militant Labour, Earth First and Glasgow For People.

The campsite was a microcosm of what people united by a shared purpose could achieve with very little resources. Macleod, a local resident who established a permanent camp in the path of the proposed road, after spending nine days in a tree to prevent it being cut down, came not only to lead the resistance but to personify its spirit, bringing purpose, connectedness and meaning into a community torn apart by poverty and political apathy.

The camp was not only a visible symbol of resistance that forced people to question the legitimacy of the power of local planners and officials, but more importantly, it became a counter-cultural lifestyle through which local people, previously blighted by low self-esteem, idleness and addiction, were upskilled and rehabilitated.

But the camp, which fluctuated in membership and comprised people of all social backgrounds, was not without its problems. As well as the locals who got involved out of a desire to influence local issues, activists and academics from outside the community flocked to the camp with broader environmental and economic concerns and this created friction. Locals often felt that the academics and students were parachuting in and taking over, ignoring or minimising their concerns and pushing their own middle class agenda of environmentalism. There were also problems with drinking and drug use in the camp and eventually alcohol and drugs were banned. In order to mitigate some of the tension between the competing interests, strict rules around non-judgemental inclusivity were established. Macleod's formidable skill as a master craftsman was eclipsed only by his natural way with people; he was intuitive, always, in how to maximise an individual's potential for the benefit of the community. He was respected by everyone and therefore able to mediate between various factions to bring about understanding.

However, the Pollok Free State was only one of a number of small but increasingly effective movements operating in the area – much to the frustration of political parties and big business. A troupe of young socialists, who would later form the Scottish Socialist Party, had become engaged by the anti poll tax movement that preceded the Pollok Free State. This was a young, vibrant and mischievous constellation of activists and community leaders.

As a result, the community began to empower itself and people previously apathetic to politics developed new instincts which they began to trust. Self-doubt, after all, is what held so many back. The belief that there's no point in trying because nobody will listen was slowly being eroded to make way for a new community confidence. The socialist activists successfully mobilised sections of the local population in service of a number of campaigns against a slew of government policies, including the closure of community centres and schools as well as 'warrant sales' – the practice of government heavies being despatched to seize household possessions for non-payment of tax.

These disparate movements, like the Pollok Free State and what would later become the Scottish Socialist Party, coalesced culturally as a renewal of community spirit that developed into a bit of a swagger. I recall a public meeting in the City Chambers where a Tory politician was so scared of the local people that he had to doodle meaningless shapes on a piece of paper to draw attention away from the fact he was visibly shaking.

Rather than lie down to the authorities, locals were occupying public land and community centres, opposing school closures. One school marked for demolition was my own, as well as another school just three miles away. Three secondary schools within a two-mile radius were to be bulldozed.

Empowered by the mischief-making in the area, teachers, staff and pupils engaged in the consultation process argued that both schools simply needed upgrading and that closure would be a massive blow to the area. They claimed the closures would effectively lead to kids being crammed into a much smaller building outside their own community. As well as my school, the main school in the neighbouring scheme, Penilee, was also to be closed, but not before the two were to be merged. The proposals, which would involve pupils being taxied between schools at intervals to attend classes being held three miles down the road, were so potentially disruptive to education that it was laughable. Education was challenging enough without this level of upheaval.

Local people and staff confidently opposed the proposals and engaged with the consultation process, certain they would force concessions from the local authority.

The wider context here was that activists had been slowly wresting responsibilities from the local authorities and assuming control of the levers of power, either democratically or otherwise, through elections or occupations. Not only were they creating a new level of political consciousness in Pollok, which inspired young and old alike, but they were also running a programme of summer activities, including live music events featuring local artists and football tournaments that brought young people together across territorial divides. Suddenly, it seemed like there were lots of positive things going on in Pollok and young people in communities that had been abandoned by successive governments were beginning to re-engage. The quality of life rose substantially, not because there was more money – there wasn't – but because people were beginning to take responsibility for their own community. In this shared purpose, our lives gained new meaning and our quality of life improved, even though our material circumstances remained the same.

But despite more than three decades of concerted push back, the M77 went ahead nonetheless, setting these opposing forces on a collision course. In one corner, you had the full might of the state at local and national level, backed by big business. In the other, an unlikely band of vegetarians, environmentalists, socialists, anarchists and recovering alcoholics and addicts. The imminent showdown was seen by many as a battle for the soul of the community.

'It's a message, man,' said Colin Macleod 'to the community around here. We know we are being watched by people, so we want to try and get their attention, let them know what is happening here, and what we are trying to protect.'

The following text is a personal journal entry from Paul Routledge the night before the diggers arrived.

People adorned with dreadlocks, shaved heads and Mohican cuts rub shoulders with people wearing kilts, tie-dyed clothes and 'ethnic wear' from various corners of the globe including India, Nepal and Guatemala. A group of musicians strike up some impromptu Celtic folk music. An air of expectancy hangs amid the wood smoke and the winter wind. The four cars that are arriving at the Free State are to be buried, engine down, in the M77 road bed alongside the five that have already been buried. Once buried, the cars will be set alight, burned as totems of resistance and on their charred skeletons anti-motorway slogans painted. Amid the sounds of car horns, whistles and cheers from the assembled crowd, the cars arrive. The cars line up beside a tree which flies the Lion Rampant. As the crowd proceeds to march towards the burial site, a band strikes up a cacophony of bagpipes, horns, drums, whistles and shouts.

We march up to the road-bed and, one by one, the cars are manoeuvred into the tombs that have been dug for them. Engine down and with earth and stones packed around them, the cars are buried vertically in the road-bed. A great cheer rises from the crowd as one teenager from the nearby Pollok housing estate hurls a stone through the driver's window, shattering the glass. A resident of the Free State swings a sledgehammer and dispenses with the windscreen. Another cheer rises from the crowd. We are a rhythmic crowd, moving to the visceral beat of the drums. We revel in the burial of the car, encoded as it is with our resistance to the environmental consequences of excessive car use and to the construction of the M77 motorway. Once the cars are buried, petrol is poured over them and they are set alight. Voices of celebration fill the air, accented with Glaswegian, London English, Australian, Swedish, American. People dance in the firelight, their shadows casting arabesques of celebration upon the road: we dance fire, we become fire, our movements are those of flames.

A steady procession of diggers, steamrollers and tractors approached the Pollok Free State, on the day construction on the

Pollok junction of the M77 was to commence, to find burnt out
cars buried in their path like gravestones; this was not only powerful symbolism, but a very stark warning that they wouldn't be
going down without a fight. The authorities had anticipated resistance and came team-handed with police as well as corporate
security. As word spread that the confrontation had commenced,
locals who were activised by the protest and were now playing
a role in their community hurried to the camp to lend whatever
hand they could.

But by the afternoon corporate muscle had literally dragged
the people of Pollok from their own land; many of them were
thrown into the back of police vans and taken to cells. These
upstarts were not to be tolerated. The totality of their lives, their
experiences and everything that had led them to this point, where
they were prepared to stand and fight for what they believed, was
regarded as no more than a vulgar impediment to the progress of
the many. The many, of course, being the people who still voted
for mainstream political parties, lived in the suburbs and disliked
long traffic queues and back roads, on their daily commute.

That day, the Pollok Free State was defeated. Not by a sworn
enemy, but by people claiming to be acting in their best interests. Whether it was the road, the closure of community centres,
schools or other services, the local authorities, while making con-
ciliatory noises to the contrary, had deliberately ignored their
wishes at every possible opportunity – because they thought they
knew better. In the tension between the concerns of locals and
the aspirations of the middle class, there would only ever be one
winner.

Within ten years, the socialist movement in Scotland, launched
from Pollok, had collapsed. A slew of community centres were
closed, demolished or mysteriously caught fire. All three local
schools, Bellarmine, Penilee and Crookston Castle, were shut
down, but not before the final humiliation of my old school being
renamed 'Penilee Annexe' – a decision so needlessly insensitive we
assumed it was made out of spite. It seemed that our culture was
not worth preserving. Or worse, that our culture was, in fact, an

absence of culture. Our ideas about how to run the area, or even what things should be called, were regarded as well-meaning but misguided. Political participation was not about the community making its voice heard, but rather, it was about corralling the herd to a pre-determined destination, decided behind closed doors.

The only thing left to be purged was the Pollok Centre, which, as Colin Macleod and others correctly predicted, became a nebula of aggressive commercialisation from which profit would be extracted from the community in return for low wages and poor working conditions. We soon learned that the Pollok Centre was to be shut down completely, as new proposals emerged to create a brand new American-style mall, filled with high-end clothing and jewellery stores, restaurants and coffee shops.

Local people were seduced by the notion that Pollok would become associated with something shiny, upmarket and respectable. For so long, Pollok had been a by-word for social deprivation. Perhaps this new multi-million-pound complex, the size of a small town, which was to be built slap bang on the junction of the new motorway where one of the schools used to be, would cultivate a new image of Pollok in the public mind. Pollok, thanks to this state-of-the-art centrepiece, would once again be regarded as a clean, safe, forward-thinking area with limitless potential that had put its gritty past behind it. People might stay for a while rather than nervously passing through. People would visit and not be ashamed to say they'd been here.

But, as it turned out, the new centre would be named 'Silverburn' – perhaps a tongue-in-cheek reference to the trolleys that used to line the banks of the river. Silverburn, a fictional consumer village superimposed on our now deformed landscape, would serve the shopping needs of people from the suburbs with disposable incomes, who could now visit our scheme without ever knowing (or having to say) they were in Pollok. Gentrification is cool when you're watching from a safe distance, but when it's your cultural history that is being dismantled, it leaves a sour taste in the mouth.

This new consumer cathedral, where many local people would

go to earn and spend their money, would soon become the talk of the town in a way Pollok could only have dreamed. Within a few years a multi-screen cinema complex and more parking space was added. Silverburn became Pollok's crowning achievement. Too bad, then, that Pollok, and by extension its people, were edited out of the success story. The political polarity of the area was completely reversed within ten years and where once locals had organised to oppose the road on which Silverburn would later be built, they were now circulating petitions demanding a McDonald's restaurant.

The only trace of our local cultural heritage can be found in a small photographic exhibition about the Pollok Centre on the wall outside the toilets. There's no mention of Colin Macleod.

10

One Flew Over the Cuckoo's Nest

WHEN YOU GROW up in the sort of community I am describing, you cannot help but be affected by it on many levels, some of them obvious and others far more subtle. The biggest impact is on your emotional life, specifically emotional stress, which plays a significant role in shaping how people think, feel and behave. The existence of emotional stress, how it affects us and what we do to manage it throughout our lives, is one of the most overlooked aspects of the poverty experience. Yet stress is often the engine room that fuels the lifestyle choices and behaviours that can lead to poor diet, addictions, mental health issues and chronic health conditions. People spend their whole lives trying to kick bad habits they know are killing them but fail because they have no insight into the role stress plays in sabotaging their good intentions.

It seems bizarre that we would ever attempt to draw conclusions about the behaviour of people in deprived communities, let alone legislate for it, without allowing for the context of stress and how that in itself is a causal factor in comfort eating, smoking, gambling, binge drinking, substance misuse and various cultures of aggression and violence. To those of you with no real insight into lower class life, these tropes may seem hard to fathom. I find them unfathomable and I've nearly done them all to death. But for people who live their lives constrained by emotional stress, anxiety or dread, such activities, while destructive in the long term, offer a brief emotional reprieve – and an illusion of control – which, when under the duress of psychological strain, creates urges, impulses and compulsions that become hard to resist. Everybody experiences stress, regardless of class, and I really can't stress this point enough. I'm not trying to minimise or dismiss the stress people from higher class backgrounds experience, nor am I saying middle class people don't suffer from stress-related problems and illnesses. But the degree to which stress inhibits our progress, harms our health and social mobility and shapes our social attitudes and values, is disproportionately high among the working classes. This must be acknowledged.

Stress in a positive setting can be a catalyst for action, a motivator; or a temporary state of discomfort. But for those living in poor social conditions, perhaps growing up in subcultures of aggression or abuse, stress is all-consuming; it's the soup everyone is swimming in all the time. Stress is the lens through which all of life is viewed. There's no specific medical definition of stress. In simple terms, stress is a physical response to psychological or emotional strain. The body believes it's under attack and alters its physiological configuration to deal with the imminent threat. This process happens automatically, outwith the realm of self-awareness, as hormones and chemicals are released to prepare it for physical action. The stress response is primitive, so even though the things we get stressed about have changed over thousands of years, our basic physical response remains the same; blood is pumped to muscles and we become adrenalised, which impairs our normal decision-making processes. Stress also changes the way the body stores energy and when stress levels are heightened, fat is stored around the gut to be used once the threat dissipates. But if you live in conditions of constant strain of the sort associated with poverty, you are always in a state of hypervigilance both mentally and physically. Stress begins to alter your physiological state.

My first real insight into this destructive emotional state, and its impact on my mind and body, came when I began attending the Notre Dame Centre in the West End of Glasgow. The Notre Dame Centre was founded in 1931 in response to the demands of parents, educators and other professionals to address the complex needs of children and young people experiencing emotional and psychological distress. Sessions lasted no more than an hour but seemed to fly in much faster. I'd arrive at the door and be greeted by a friendly, warm-hearted woman named Moira. Like the school dinner ladies, I always got the sense that she was happy to see me and we'd often resume previous conversations once I was signed in. She would congratulate me on my activities (outwith my counselling) which had come to her attention: recent media appearances, occurring with increasing frequency, in which I was invited on radio to talk about poverty. Now I had two reasons to be in the West End and was making something of a habit of being on this side of town.

In the waiting area the radio played chart music and kids, either with family members or support workers, passed the time thumbing through lifestyle magazines. But this didn't feel like a typical doctor's surgery. It was a little more unpredictable. Sometimes you'd see adults, presumably professionals, trailing kids around the building, often engaged in negotiation with them. Other times you would hear shouting or banging from the next room, or see someone running out of the building, upset. These occasions were not regular, but when they did occur there was a sense that nothing out of the ordinary was happening. Staff were used to this kind of environment and dealing with traumatised children with complex mental health problems was obviously part of their job description. In the reception room, I'd sit, tapping my toe, waiting to be called by my psychologist, Marilyn. The session usually took place in a quiet, dimly lit room on the first floor of the building. Marilyn was of average height with short brown hair that curled up at her shoulders. She was bright-eyed and had a good sense of humour, and I immediately felt comfortable the first time we met. If I recall correctly, my auntie attended the first session with me, but thereafter I went to the Notre Dame Centre alone.

The first problem she wanted to help me get to the bottom of was why I felt so angry. She asked me to describe where in my body this anger resided and what, if any, physical sensations accompanied it. Without hesitation, I placed my right hand on my chest and described it unambiguously as a 'ball of fire'. For me,

2001 was a very difficult year and life at home became unliveable. My dad and I were not on speaking terms, so I was surprised when he called me, early in March. It was a brief phone call, fraught with tension, in which he informed me that my mum was unwell and had been hospitalised. It was difficult to glean any more information from him due to the strained nature of our relationship. The miscommunication was worsened by the fact my mother was a compulsive liar, often concocting mystery illnesses and dramas to explain her unreliability. On the rare occasion that she did call to speak to us, she was inebriated and eventually I simply refused to talk to her. As I got older my attitude towards her softened slightly, thanks to my dad encouraging me to speak to her, which I'd often refuse to do, and tried to convince my siblings to follow suit. Shortly before I was invited to leave the family home, she made a surprise call. For the first time in years, she sounded sober.

Funnily enough, I was in my dad's room, writing and recording a song about her. She seemed interested in what I was doing, which for me was a rare treat as I'd never experienced that quality of interaction with her. She even asked me questions about the song. I told her I didn't want to give it away but that I would let her hear it once it was finished. The track was a story about growing up around her drinking, but written with empathy and forgiveness. For me, beginning to see her as a sick person, as opposed to a bad one, was a breakthrough. I'd spent so many years of my childhood cursing her name, even wishing death upon her, that to finally make peace with her alcoholism filled me with hope that we could salvage a relationship. In truth, I dreamed of helping her recover. But by the end of the month she was dead.

Because of the confusion around her condition and the strained relationship between me and my father, we were denied the opportunity to visit her in hospital. We were later told this was because she was in such a delirious state, with advanced cirrhosis of the liver, that she wouldn't have recognised us. That was little consolation. Personally, I'd rather have seen her, distressing as that may have been, if only to lay eyes on her one last time before she passed. As her son this was my right, and to be denied the chance to hold my own mother's hand before she died was extremely upsetting.

This made me angry.

Marilyn, intuitive to my needs, taught me how to manage powerful emotions like anger when they surfaced, rather than seek to avoid them. She encouraged me to face them as and when they arose. She helped lend context to the emotional disturbances that would engulf and disorientate me, offering me insight into their origin and reminding me that I need not identify with every thought that popped into my head – especially the ones about taking my own life. I continued to attend the Notre Dame Centre and, as well as learning techniques to cope with my emotions, I also began having flashbacks and memories from much earlier in my childhood. Some were vague and difficult to verify, like being dangled out of a window by my legs late at night. My time with Marilyn became a journey into my own subconscious, where I'd discover many things I'd spend the following decade drinking to forget.

One memory involved being sent out by my mum, during a gale-force storm, to get cigarettes from her mother (my other granny), who lived across from the high flats in low-level accommodation. I remember telling her that I was scared to go outside because of the storm. The next thing I recall is being at the foot of the building, which was a wind trap even in moderate weather, and peering around the corner to see parked cars tilting slightly as the gale got beneath them. Still, I had no choice but to run the errand, so I braved the storm and stepped out into the wide-open space between the two buildings. But as I walked forward, the wind started to get under me too. It was frightening to feel such a force behind me and I was scared that I was going to get hurt, yet I had no choice but to keep going. My mistake was to try and run, hoping to get it over quicker, which led to me being blown off my feet and rolling along the concrete. When I came to a stop, my jacket torn, I turned to the tower block my mum lived in, gesturing for help, only to see her and her boyfriend looking out, laughing at me. For years this painful memory had concealed itself in some dark corner of my brain. Suddenly my conscious mind was flooding with bits and pieces of events, or fullblown flashbacks such as the one just described. Bits and pieces of memories that felt like dreams began fighting their way into my waking mind, bringing with them difficult questions and deep emotional disturbances.

Another flashback involved our old dog, Kelly, who was killed by a motorbike. Later that night my dad had buried her at the bottom of the garden. My mother was devastated. The next day, having spent the night drinking, she was drunk and inconsolable. She emerged from upstairs, incoherent, staggered around the living room and then proceeded to the back garden where, to our absolute horror, she attempted to dig Kelly up with her bare hands. She turned, her arms outstretched, begging me to help, before plunging her long fingers back into the dirt as neighbours stared on in disbelief. Who knows how I could have forgotten such a thing? Then again, when you consider how shocking something like that is to read, imagine what it was like to witness. There are some things a young mind simply cannot process and memories like these are sent directly to storage to be accessed at a later date.

It soon became clear that my psychological state was not merely a direct result of my mother's sudden passing, but of everything that occurred prior to her death. I continued to see Marilyn, on and off, for a year. In 2002, she referred me to the Firestation Project: a service which offered 'housing support for young, vulnerable adults aged 16–25 years, who are or have been homeless or are at risk of homelessness'. My housing status was precarious: living between friends and family members and, increasingly, with my new girlfriend – though our relationship was already showing signs of dysfunction. Marilyn believed the Firestation Project would give me an opportunity to focus on the emotional difficulties I was facing. Without the threat of homelessness hanging over my head, I'd be better able to address the issues that were emerging around my early years and how those experiences were beginning to shape me as an adult.

Marilyn had a fundamental influence on the direction of my life, one that remains to this day. Without her intervention, I doubt whether I would have developed the self-awareness to zoom out of my disordered thinking and see my stress in a broader context. Not only did she provide me with insight and practical tools, like meditation, to help me understand and regulate my emotions, but she also became a much needed source of continuity in the chaos of my life. She, along with my gran, was someone I could depend on and trust. Despite my increasing unreliability, I rarely missed appointments with Marilyn and always felt lifted and energised following our sessions. If I'm honest, I grew very fond of her. I felt she was in my corner. I felt supported, heard and understood by her. With Marilyn, I felt a nurturing human connection which seemed to quieten my stress and anxiety, and the isolating or disruptive urges they would trigger in me. However, while I attribute much of this crucial intervention to Marilyn, the fact is that she was a professional, employed by an organisation set up to provide a public service.

But whereas before I had only accessed public services in times of need, now, on the verge of becoming homeless, I was about to start living in one.

11

A Tale of Two Cities

PEOPLE END UP homeless for all sorts of reasons. However, just like those who end up in prison, one recurring factor in the lives of those who become residentially challenged is family breakdown or dysfunction. Issues like child abuse, addiction and homelessness are often discussed in isolation, but as anyone working with homeless people, addicts or victims of abuse will tell you, the problems are often interconnected.

I became homeless at the age of 18 after a psychological breakdown, following my mother's death. Her own life was cut short by drink and drug addiction. In fact, she too was homeless not long before she died at 36 years of age. We both ended up homeless because of problems that stemmed from family dysfunction. It's in these highly stressful conditions that vulnerable families break down and people find themselves without a place to call their own. When you find yourself unleashed on the world, it really is a matter of luck what sort of crowd you end up in. Fortunately, I was referred to a supported accommodation project where I lived for three years and never had to sleep rough. Life in the Firestation Project was very a real gear shift from life as a regular civilian. There was constant staff support. It was very rare that at least one member of staff wasn't in the downstairs office. Sometimes there would be a whole team working at the same time. The three-storey tenement building stood in the shadow of high-rises. My flat was on the top floor looking out onto a busy street. From my window, I could glimpse a bit of the city skyline behind more flats across the road. On the ground floor there was the common room where I had my interview to secure a flat, and this was a great space. But it was rarely used except for the tense monthly tenants' meeting, when we'd all be forced out of our reclusion and into a room with one another for 25 minutes. Outside the door of the common room was a public phone but it was rarely in use, due to people smashing it in anger or breaking into it for cash. At the bottom of the long and winding staircase, to the left, were the staff office and living quarters.

Back then, the welfare system seemed flush with cash. Or at least, controls on money were not as strict as they are now. I remember being quite surprised by all the benefits I was told I was entitled to. Before moving in, I had been doing agency work as a kitchen porter, then bingo-calling at the Pollok Centre. But as my mental health deteriorated I found jobs harder to hold down. A day would always come when I was so full of fear that the thought of speaking to another person would force me into hiding.

The first thing that happened when I moved into the Firestation Project was an initial assessment when I met with my support workers to discuss the nature of my problems. Everything from my mental and physical health to my income and outgoings was logged. The average duration of a tenant at the Firestation Project was under two years – I remained there for nearly three. The first task for my support workers was to stabilise my income by identifying my benefit entitlement. The strategy consisted of applying for everything that I could conceivably get. Within a few weeks, I was on income support and housing benefit – meaning I didn't have to sign on any more – and an application for Disability Living Allowance was also made, though this took much longer to process. I don't remember filling out any forms, I only remember them being brought to me to sign and everything else being dealt with on my behalf.

The staff here were like Marilyn. They were passionate about the work they did and they made me feel valued. My support workers were positive forces in my life. They encouraged me to develop my talents as well as work through my problems and they challenged me whenever they felt it was necessary. I'm still amazed at the quality of the time they gave me, considering how overwhelmed the project was at certain points. Only a month in the door and I found myself on a foreign holiday, organised by the project, which I paid for partly thanks to my granny but also because the Notre Dame Centre offered to double whatever I could raise. I went away with less than everyone else but it was enough for me. I didn't know any of the other tenants and was still finding my feet. I think about ten of us went on the trip and by the end of the first night we were rolling about the beaches fighting in the wee hours of the morning, screaming at each other in hotels or at the poolside and drinking far too much in extremely high temperatures. By the end of the first week I wanted to come home. It soon dawned on me that I was in some troubled company, though it hadn't occurred to me that I might be just as troubled too. I coped by pretending I was less messed up than everyone else. Within weeks I purchased my first pack of cigarettes, within a year I was drinking every other day.

I was now receiving hundreds of pounds a week in benefits as well as two massive back payments for DLA after an application process that took over 12 months. The backdated amount alone was nearly £5,000. I had never seen so much money in my life. I remember lying to my family that the money was from sales from my first album (which was funded with a grant from the Prince's Trust) because I didn't want them to know I was getting disability benefits. I was ashamed. Whenever I'd see family I would try and talk up all the cool things I was doing and underemphasise the problems I was experiencing. It was in the Firestation Project that I first recall purchasing alcohol, just so I had it in the house. At the time, I remember thinking I had crossed a line but I put it out of my mind. What I didn't realise was that this was a feature of addiction; the minimising of the truth and the postponement of action. That day I hadn't even bought it to consume but simply to have there, like a friend. Later, this would be the flat where I would experience my first comedown from ecstasy, roll my first joint and try my first Valium.

By the time I left that place, I was drunk every other day

and using party drugs like ecstasy, cocaine and speed as well as powerful downers like jellies, nitrazepam and ketamine. But even though I was in receipt of such high rates of benefit and getting my rent paid (which went directly to the landlord), I still couldn't budget to keep up payments of £5 to utilities companies for gas and electricity. My financial and living situation had been stabilised initially, thanks to staff at the project, but my life quickly descended into chaos because of my drinking and drug use. Strangely, during this time the issue of my drinking was not identified by staff or health professionals. It wasn't even identified by me. My alcohol and substance misuse was not something I was attempting to conceal at this point. I had so little insight into what an issue it was that I didn't even consider the role it was playing in my circumstances. I was in such denial that I didn't even think it was a problem. Instead, I was presenting with symptoms of mental illness and these became the focus of all the staff I interacted with, across a broad range of services.

I had a psychologist, a psychiatrist, a cognitive behavioural therapist, two support workers and a neurolinguistics programmer. I was experiencing a wide range of symptoms that resembled mental illnesses like severe depression, bipolar disorder and even schizophrenia, but a diagnosis always eluded me. Sometimes I would hallucinate, hear voices or become paralysed in my sleep and then experience vivid nightmares while I lay there paralysed. On DLA and surrounded by professionals, I started to see myself as a sick person with serious mental health problems beyond my own control. This continued long after I left the Firestation when, after a further year of drinking and getting high, I became homeless again. But rather than accept I had a drink and drug problem, I became fixated on the idea I was mentally ill. Of course, I was, but not in the way I believed.

I ended up staying in a friend's place but his flat was more like a squat; he slept on his couch and only really lived in one room – the others were filled with dust and junk. One night, when I had been sitting in the living room drinking with a couple of friends, someone arrived at the door. It was another pal of ours. He was

going through a bit of a cocaine binge but was one of those high
functioning drug users I envied. He could snort a couple of grams
and get up for work the next day, no problem. He must have been
getting bored of snorting lines and decided he wanted to switch
things up a bit, so he had brought a few grams round to ask our
mate – a recovering heroin addict – to show him how to turn it
into crack. Our friend obliged. To my surprise he even smoked
it, despite apparently being off hard drugs. Before I knew what
was happening, a pipe was being passed around and everyone
was smoking crack. As the pipe got closer to me I began to panic;
another line was about to be crossed, this time into harder drugs
than I'd ever tried. I had heard the stories about how much of a
rush a crack hit was, but also how addictive it could be. Given
the fact I had ended up abusing every substance I had tried, from
refined sugar to ketamine, the chances of me only smoking crack
once were pretty slim.

I sipped from my bottle manically, trying not to appear scared
in front of my mates, who were all much older than me, but I was
terrified. What was so frightening was my sense of powerlessness.
I knew if it was passed to me I couldn't say no, even though I
didn't really want to do it. I thought of my mum and the rooms
she used to sit in during the day, drinking or injecting. I thought
of that squalor and the lines that were crossed by so many people
in those dark days. It suddenly hit me that this situation I now
found myself in was the same. I realised that this was how most
other people happened upon hard drugs. Not in dark, rat-infested
high-rises, but in the rooms of people they called friends. People
don't go out searching for crack or heroin, they often stumble
upon it through a social circle they become part of when they
are experiencing personal problems. People are often handed
the drugs that kill them by friends they love deeply. In these
circumstances, the drugs are not seen as the problem, the pain
is. Through a mix of peer pressure and natural curiosity, people
decide to try something once and for many it soon becomes a
habit. It was surreal to be aware of the significance of what was
going on yet still feel unable to resist. But when the pipe was

about to be passed to me something happened: the buzzer for the door went and everybody freaked out and stashed the stuff.

That day I dodged a bullet. But so many others don't. The reason these drugs are so appealing is that they are often destitute and miserable when they are presented with them. It's easy to talk in platitudes about the homeless and drug users, but that's all your observations are until you've really seen this stuff up close. It was when I was homeless that I become most vulnerable to the dangers around me. Poverty, despite what felt like my best efforts, had me firmly in its grip. Despite three years in supported accommodation, I could only escape its gravitational field via delusions or through chemical inebriation. Now in my mid-20s, nearly ten years after I left Pollok, I was slowly turning into everything I had hated and feared as a child. No matter where I went, the tower blocks of the Gorbals cast a long and ominous shadow over my life.

12

Wuthering Heights

IT'S THE EIGHTH rainy day of May in the year 2016 and I still haven't smoked crack. The sun, despite a weatherman's prediction, has yet to make an appearance. It's lurking nervously behind a thick curtain of grey cloud as a crowd gathers for today's matinee show. Staring up at the solitary tower block of Norfolk Court, in the Gorbals, it's hard to imagine that this unsightly structure, which now imposes like an unwelcome guest on its newly gentrified surroundings, was once pitched as a New York style skyscraper that would revolutionise social housing.

The term 'gentrification' simply means people with more money than you, but not more money than people with money, are being invited to set up shop in your area on the cheap, in the hope that their presence will lift you a little out of the gutter. When you're sitting in an artisan café called Soy Division, in the middle of a slum, and there is a toddler named Wagner eating tofu off the floor, that's gentrification. It's the new word for regeneration, or rather, it's the gentrification of regeneration.

Today we are about to witness another aspect of gentrification, namely, the practice of getting rid of any evidence that the community is working class. That, of course, increases the chances of people with a bit more money moving in. I don't mean to sound bitter or cynical, but I am, so that's just how it comes out. In a few moments, Norfolk Court will be destroyed in a controlled explosion; the last of a quartet in this part of the community over the last few years. A few hundred yards to the left, Norfolk's sister towers, Stirlingfauld Place and Court, are but a distant memory, having been demolished years earlier. I have a personal connection to this part of town because it's where my mother grew up. When she left the family home in the early '90s, she returned here to live in a flat in Stirlingfauld Place. Hers was one that the stereotype is based on. When I see a tower block, sometimes I think of her.

Moments before the signal is given, there is a sense of calm anticipation among the locals gathered to watch the demolition. For some, this is the end of an era as the last remnants of their childhoods are pulled, like rotten teeth, from the visible horizon. For others, this is an elaborate piece of urban theatre, a live art installation marking the onset of a new phase of social progress. For everyone else, it's that rare occasion in the calendar when there's something interesting to do. In its final moments, there is a defiant pride about the tower as it holds up stubbornly, like a middle finger to modernity. Despite its unsightliness, there is dignity in the old ruin as it lingers, swaying in the clouds with a quiet grace, wrongly condemned for someone else's crime. Given how unceremoniously the icons of their lives are wiped from local memory, it's not hard to see why so many people roll their eyes whenever they hear the word 'regeneration'. The very homes they grew up in and played around as children, perhaps before raising families of their own, are often remembered only as terrible mistakes; embarrassing blemishes which had to be erased from the city skyline.

Within seconds the explosives are triggered, inviting gasps and then cheers from the crowd. The spectators look on in wonder as the hollowed-out structure comes apart like flakes of snow before collapsing into its own footprint at freefall speed. There, it finally rests as a thick cloud of dust moves out towards the onlookers. It's no surprise that successive generations of people, who call this building site home, have internalised and perpetuated the negative narratives and urban myths about their community being a dump. Many sincerely believe that things will never change. Given how frequently this community has been reduced to rubble in the last century, it's hard to contest such a view.

For those who don't have emotional roots here, these flats represent a blip in social progress; an unfortunate but necessary misstep in order that we learn how to do it properly next time. Their failure presents an opportunity to learn, to innovate and to develop. Though such an observation, if made indiscreetly, may appear insensitive or even offensive to the people who live here. Regeneration exposes the ravine between the people who see this community as a 'project' or a 'scheme', an ongoing enterprise or a problem to solve and the people who actually live here. Of course, it's important to be objective and not overly sentimental but the reality for people who live in areas like this is all-consuming. People have neither the luxury nor the inkling to zoom out from their own lives and view their run-down communities in the broader context of social progress.

It's an understatement to say that many have become angry, disillusioned or apathetic after years of feeling ignored, dismissed and bullied by agencies and institutions speaking in the mechanical jargon of regeneration. There's a feeling in sections of these communities, among those who want to actively participate, that things are not done *with* the community but *to* it. Much like the school curriculum, where your value is derived not only from your ability to think and reason but also from your willingness to submit to a process, the conversation about decision-making in your own community follows a similar pattern. You must engage within the parameters set by the people who are really in charge. If you fail to do so, you risk becoming a pariah. Or at least that is how many locals feel. Even assuming nobody wants it to be this way, the social gulf between many of the decision-makers and the people who live here is so wide that people woefully misread one another's intentions. Thankfully, about half a mile from the rubble of Norfolk Court, the green shoots of a less sceptical future are clear to see – for anyone who takes the time to look.

13

The Outsiders

GATHERED NEATLY ON some tarmac, a group of around 15 children wait patiently outside a local community centre called The Barn. They seem cheerful for a Monday evening. As they rub their hands together, one might assume it's to ward off the winter chill, but it's far more likely in anticipation of the arrival of the youth workers who will soon open the doors.

'Coming to The Barn geez me peace, it gets me oot the hoose', says 12-year-old Benji, with enviable self-awareness.

As the doors swing open and the young people scramble inside, a youth worker smiles: 'They're at the door all the time. They come here right after school. But we don't have the staff to keep the place open.'

Life in the Gorbals is in a state of transition. Unlike other parts of Glasgow, where progress occurs incrementally, if at all, here on the south bank of the Clyde, change is palpable and dramatic. The term 'regeneration' has become a byword for opportunism, mismanagement and exploitation, a fancy word of no real consequence. Like the shrill birds that scout the area, defecating from a height before flying off with whatever scraps they find, decision-making in places like the Gorbals is a messy, top-down business, conducted over the heads of the people who live here. In communities like this it has created a fertile bed of resentment from which anger and apathy have grown.

But you wouldn't know from talking to these kids.

The interior of The Barn is brightly lit and colourfully deco-rated. Life affirming slogans adorn the walls. One reads: 'Don't aim for success if you want it; just do what you love and believe in, and it will come naturally.' Situated in the middle on the main hall are funkily coloured couches where teenagers – who recently constituted their own youth committee – chat, while the younger kids dart around between air hockey, table tennis, pool, snooker, baking, football and even a sectioned off computer room for Xbox enthusiasts.

In The Barn, local young people of all ages and abilities learn how to play, share and express themselves in a safe and affirming environment. But all this has to be paid for, which means it must be quantified, measured and justified every 12 months, or it may become subject to 'efficiency savings'.

Joe McConnell, the recognised leader (he asks me not to refer to him as a manager), believes there is an inverse relationship between what politicians say they want to happen in these communities and what they actually do: 'There does still seem to be not a great deal of will for longer term investment in young people and the development of so-called soft skills. There is a discrepancy at government level between the desires for the kind of society we want to live in and the resources that are allocated to help this happen and where they are directed.'

Joe's comments are unusually frank in a sector where there is a culture of sweeping certain issues under the rug. Regeneration is not just a benign and benevolent social programme designed to improve the lives of the poor, it's also an industry with many pathways to career progression. Self-interest plays a decisive role in how business is conducted – even if many in the sector are in denial about it. This has a cooling effect where a certain form of criticism is concerned. In fact, criticism itself, like many other aspects of the community, is carefully managed; fed into an 'evaluation process', which, like the planning process, often leaves local people locked out or invited to take part in some contrived or tokenistic way. When people are critical in a manner deemed to be inappropriate they are told to be 'more constructive' – usually by someone not from the community. That point might seem like an irrelevance to some. But if somebody you didn't recognise was suddenly to appear in your area, with what looked like resources and a bit of authority, and proceeded to chastise you about the way you talk about the problems in your own community, you would likely feel insulted.

Of course, being constructive is important but sometimes this trope is invoked as an evasion tactic. Therefore, it is perceived (whether intentional or not), as a display of power which only aggravates the gaping class wound at the centre of the tension. The question people who are being told to be more constructive will inevitably ask is: 'If this is our community, then who has the authority to say what is and isn't constructive?'

Joe's straight talk regarding some of the problems in the sector is unusual because when you work in communities like this, and are dependent on money from further up the food chain, you quickly develop an instinct for what you should and shouldn't say. These instincts for self-preservation manifest, collectively, as the professional orthodoxy; the accepted way of doing things. Over time, this way of doing things, which coincidentally aligns with the interests of the people working in the sector, often gets confused with what's good for the community. People who turn a blind eye to this tend to go further than those who point it out. Joe is not alone in his frustration with community economics. There is a constant murmur of resentment in deprived communities among those who feel overlooked, bypassed and usurped when temporary hierarchies are installed. These organisations are usually acting on behalf of central government though give the appearance of autonomous institutions. This sector, which comprises arts, the media, charities, and NGOs, behaves much like an imperial power; poorer communities are viewed as primitive cultures that need to be modernised, retooled and upskilled. Not necessarily a bad thing, this approach is often predicated on the assumption that people in these communities don't have any ideas of their own. That they exist in a cultural and political vacuum with no past or future. For locals who wish to engage, it leads to a sense that privileged people with little insight into their concerns are being parachuted in to superimpose their values onto everyone. Projects that are rolled out in this way are less about identifying the community's shared aspiration than about deciding what the community needs and then corralling, manipulating or compelling people towards it.

Truth be told, much of the work carried out in deprived communities is as much about the aims and objectives of the organisations facilitating it as it is about local needs. And notably, the aim is rarely to encourage self-sufficiency. Rather the opposite, each engagement and intervention creating more dependency on outside resources and expertise, perpetuating the role of the sector as opposed to gradually reducing it.

These assumptions, which filter through much of the work being carried out, create the conditions for multi-million pound projects to become mired in power struggles and community apathy as locals feel no sense of connection to what is going on. This can lead to potentially life-changing work falling hopelessly out of sync with grassroots needs and aspirations, particularly when the work being carried out is conceived at executive level and makes very little sense in the community itself. This is as true of social housing in poor communities as it is of many arts and drama projects. When the money is made available from government, with stipulations about how it should be spent, this sector simply throws out everything it was doing previously and makes for the low-hanging fruit – regardless of what the communities they purport to serve really need or want. In these areas, poor people are viewed as a form of capital; containers from which data and narrative are extracted to justify and perpetuate the roles of the organisations charged with managing their lives. It's a steady procession of well-meaning students, academics and professionals, descending into the bowels of poverty, taking what they need before retreating to their enclaves to examine the artefacts they retrieved on the safari.

The massive multi-agency structures that have emerged to address the social problems created by industrial decline have become a problematic industry in themselves. Worse still, they are increasingly subordinate to government when they would function far better as a check on centralised power. Criticism of government policy is muted from this sector and the parameters for discussion on issues like child poverty are limited – unless it's politically expedient to expand them. Many of these organisations, dependent on government to survive, become such vast bureaucracies that they are rendered inflexible and unresponsive to what is really going on in the communities they are paid so handsomely to serve.

Organisations like The Barn in the Gorbals, or PEEK in the Calton, or Fuse in Shettleston, are well-run grassroots groups that are known and loved by locals. Despite the level of experience and expertise they bring to the table, they are constantly having to repurpose and redefine themselves in accordance with the political whims of the day. This while competing with massive organisations and institutions, like the council, that don't have a clue what they're doing.

Joe seems exhausted with having to explain why The Barn's work is important. While often misunderstood in certain quarters or seen as an indulgence, Joe claims good youth work 'can have a profound and positive effect on young people and it is a challenging and hugely rewarding job. But I think we are a long way from this being understood or accepted by a fairly large element of funding bodies and the public sector. There is funding out there for specific targets, outcomes and issues. However, many of these are not relevant to the work we do. The identity crisis within the sector does not help this situation'. Joe is clearly the sort of no-nonsense person that a bureaucrat would rather kept his mouth shut.

'We are working to combat the effects that inequality and poverty has on the lives of young people,' he says. 'The cycle of insecurity, mistrust, lack of resilience, low self-esteem and confidence. It is holistic, long term and multi-faceted work.'

Barry McLaughlin, a 28-year-old youth worker formerly employed at The Barn, feels improving self-esteem, and not simply employability, is key to cultivating the kind of self-belief and resilience which eludes so many young people in areas like the Gorbals. Young people who come to see themselves as faulty and defective, like so many of the hollowed-out structures around them.

Refreshingly unguarded, Barry says, 'The most important thing for us is the positive relationships you build up with the young people. If you don't have trust, then nothing can be achieved.' He continues: 'There's a sense of apathy due to decisions being made in the Gorbals without consulting the people that live here. The Gorbals has a negative narrative that says "We're not good enough." We're trying to change that by saying the Gorbals is an amazing place. The tools to fix the place are already here rather than parachuting government initiatives in who don't understand the area. They want us to do work that looks good and sounds good; but isn't always good.'

Barry, visibly concerned he might be neglecting the young people merely by talking to me, says: 'Impact is something we are asked about a lot by funders but it's difficult to quantify. You can see it as soon as you walk in the door.'

Joe and his team are one of many small organisations that are dealing with the social and cultural legacy of decades of poor planning and tokenistic consultation with local people. This legacy has resulted in successive generations growing up in social deprivation and all the disadvantage it implies, with a deeply held belief that they have no stake in or control over anything in their lives. Rather than learn these lessons, and learn to trust local people and involve them, another layer of managers and mentors has been added to conceal the fact the conversation is still being centrally controlled. But no matter how you dress it up, people can sense when they are being patronised. They know who is really in charge, which is why many, after an initial enthusiasm to participate, become sceptical and disengaged.

This perceived lack of control or stake in anything works in conjunction with a permanently stressful social environment to create the conditions for futile, self-defeating behaviour which, in high concentrations, can blight lives and lead to social exclusion. Joe and Barry provide a service that has the potential to interrupt this stream of needless inevitability. They can provide a sense of continuity in a young person's life, like Marilyn did in mine, that may not be possible at home. The Barn presents the opportunity to forge meaningful connections with these young people, before they go off the rails, but this work is often hindered – and undermined – by the very organisations and institutions financed to empower and enfranchise them. Unfortunately, there is no constructive way of broaching the topic without upsetting or offending people in this sector.

This is the poverty industry, where even the good guys make a mint from social deprivation. Where success is when there remain just enough social problems to sustain and perpetuate everyone's career. Success is not eradicating poverty but parachuting in and leaving a 'legacy'. And when you up and leave, withdrawing your resources and expertise as you go, if a legacy hasn't materialised, one is simply fabricated. In this sector, the orthodoxy is to deny that this is happening. The way of doing things is to turn a blind eye. Nobody can admit when they fail or if things don't work because everyone is terrified of getting their funding cut. Yet there is resentment (and even indignance) in some quarters towards those of us who have the temerity to point these things out.

Before rejoining the kids in the body of the hall, Barry sighs: 'In an ideal world we would get funded for building trusting relationships with young people.' Maybe one day he will. It's a task which, I can assure you, is not as easy – or simple – as it sounds.

14

The Trick is to Keep Breathing

IT'S THE HEIGHT of summer and the local library is full of kids waiting to take part in today's playgroup. There are about 20 children between the ages of five and 12, evenly split between male and female. Not long after the activities get under way, one girl, visibly nervous, removes herself from the group and is now sitting beside me. She is new. I speculate that she has taken herself away from the other kids because she is shy, but as the kids give some random bursts of excitable cheering, the little girl places her hands over her ears, frightened by the noise. She is visibly stressed by the sound of the other children having fun.

I notice she is wearing make-up, which, while not a red flag, is quite unusual because she is only ten years old. I make small talk by asking her where she comes from and it isn't long before she begins to divulge what is really going on. Despite not knowing me, she is overcome by an urge to disclose intimate details of her life. This urge is common among victims of abuse and neglect who, burdened by trauma, seek to purge themselves of painful memories and events by vomiting them up to anyone who will listen. It may also, in evolutionary terms, be a survival mechanism that is activated when the child is at risk of harm.

She discloses, in a very matter-of-fact way, that her dad is in prison because he gets angry and that she and her mother have been trying to get away from him. She tells me he has a loud voice and that he is scary. I notice how she can talk and draw simultaneously but that her make-up has been poorly applied – likely because she did it herself. In my role as a 'learning assistant', I should now be recording her comments with the intention of informing a child protection officer so that this little girl's situation is logged in some way. However, knowing the system as well as I do, I also know that this may place more stress on the family, thus exacerbating the conditions in which they appear to be living. We continue talking while I assess, internally, the best course of action, until our conversation is interrupted by another girl, who is crying. I ask her what is wrong.

'I miss my mummy,' she replies, tears streaming down her face.

I ask her to sit down. She does, snivelling, as the other girl resumes colouring her picture. I turn to the girl who is crying and ask her where she is from. 'Bearsden', she replies, in a polite accent. Bearsden is an affluent community on the outskirts of Glasgow. It's unusual for children from that part of town to be over here. Put simply, we deal mainly with children from poor sections of the community who tend to access our services because they are free. For this reason, it is not unsurprising that she feels scared in this unfamiliar environment.

'How did you end up at this club?' I ask.

'I was staying at my cousins,' she says, pointing them out in the melee as her breathing returns to normal.

This little girl is also stressed but for a different reason. She is stressed because it is unusual for her to be separated from her mother, who has only just left the club 20 minutes prior. She is upset and frightened, but it's less likely because of abuse at home (though I could be wrong) and more likely due to the fact she is accustomed to feeling secure. She is so used to being taken care of by her mother that being separated from her for half an hour fills her with enough dread to elicit tears.

Meanwhile, the little girl in make-up, lost in her colouring book, is well adjusted to feelings of insecurity. She has already adapted to the reality that her life is frightening. Despite suffering abuse – verbal and psychological at the very least – as well as emotional neglect, she has yet to shed a tear, despite being visibly stressed. One girl has an expectation of danger and the other an expectation of security. Both expectations are correct, based on their respective experiences in life; however, both expectations now place them at odds with the situation they now find themselves in. One girl feels scared, despite being safe, the other stressed while the rest of the kids are having fun.

Subjectively, these girls are experiencing equally uncomfortable emotions, but the wider context, social environment and emotional history is vastly different. It's at least arguable that the physiological difference between these two children, even at this young age, is rooted in social inequality. In the case of the little girl in the make-up, the trauma she has experienced may already be impairing her ability to assess risk and regulate emotions. Her hypervigilance has made her sensitive to the noise of children playing, which she wrongly interprets as a threat. This false belief is already having a profound impact on her ability to socialise and connect, creating an isolation urge. Canadian physician Gabor Maté, who specialises in addiction, trauma and neurology, describes how trauma and neglect can impact victims by reframing the world as a dangerous and frightening place. In his book *In the Realm of Hungry Ghosts,* he writes:

> The greatest damage done by neglect, trauma or emotional loss is not the immediate pain they inflict but the long term distortions they induce in the way a developing child will continue to interpret the world and her situation in it. All too often these ill-conditioned, implicit beliefs become self-fulfilling prophecies in our lives. Unwittingly, we write the story of our future from narratives based on the past. Choice begins the moment you disidentify from the mind and its conditioned patterns, the moment you become present.

This observation could, of course, apply equally to both girls as they progress through their lives. We all project false beliefs about ourselves and the world into the future. However, the girl in make-up, from the less privileged social background stands to struggle more when her false beliefs begin to interact with precarious social circumstances, creating the conditions for sustained emotional stress. If she interprets children playing in a safe environment as a threat, then you must wonder, under what conditions could she possibly relax and feel safe? Much as she has decided to remove herself from a group of children playing, she might carry that isolation urge into adolescence and adulthood, where different expectations and stresses are placed on her and, crucially, where a different set of solutions become available.

The second these girls leave the playgroup their lives will continue to diverge, as they have done since the day they were born; their respective social environments and how they impact upon them psychologically, emotionally, socially and culturally, are likely to produce two very different people. These differences may find expression in everything – their behaviour, their mental and physical state, education and life opportunities as well as their social values, political views, cultural interests and preferences and even the way they speak. These differences may also play a role in what sort of relationships they form, the lifestyles they adopt, how often they will travel and the health problems they have later in life. Even their respective lifespans are likely to reflect this inequality.

In 20 years' time, the gulf in their experiences will probably mean that the chance of them ever interacting again is slim. They'll exist in two distinct parallel cultures between which it's very difficult to move. I'd even wager that, should they cross paths in the future and attempt to communicate on a matter of substance for any prolonged period, they will be antagonised by one another on a number of levels. They will begin to judge each other based on appearance, voice, accent, language and tone. These judgements will occur subconsciously, as they attempt to engage in conversation, until eventually they hit a juncture at which there is a difference of opinion. Having subconsciously made their assessments of one another, based on their own distinct experiences and the social and cultural attitudes and expectations these have created, it is likely that they will misunderstand one another so fundamentally that they'll walk away from the interaction abruptly, feeling deeply offended or insulted by what the other person appears to imply.

One may conclude that the other is small-minded, vulgar, aggressive and intimidating, while herself being seen as mollycoddled, judgemental or spoiled. Two girls, who once attended the same playgroup, now separated by a gulf of experience so vast that simply speaking to one another has the potential to create so much confusion, ill feeling and resentment that it becomes easier to retreat to familiarity.

The familiarity of their class.

15

The Cutting Room

NOW LET'S CONDUCT a little experiment. Up until now you've been enduring anecdotal ranting or shameless personal testimony from me that's designed to elicit a strong emotional response. By now, you are hopefully deeply involved in this story about my family and me. Which is why now would be a perfect time to turn it all on its head. Instead of me testifying my experience, for it to be dissected by academics and professionals before being fed into a bank of exclusive knowledge, how about I take a wee shot of being the expert? I mean, I know I'm not an expert and I know you know I'm not an expert but, well, this is my book. There's no way someone like me would have been given the opportunity to write a book like this had I not draped it, at least partially, in the veil of a misery memoir. Okay then, first, we need to create the illusion of objectivity. It seems the most effective way to do this would be to completely dehumanise my family and me, to look at our experience through a statistical lens. Having heard so much personal testimony, let's now turn my four siblings and me into quantifiable data for your rational consideration. This process should facilitate the sort of objectivity that is necessary to scientifically assess the issue. Here we go:

Four out of five have experienced alcohol or substance misuse problems at some point.
Three have a criminal record.
Five have experienced long term financial problems which involve debilitating debt or defaults and poor credit history.
Three were suspended or excluded from school for disruptive

or violent behaviour.

Two have attempted suicide on one or more occasion.

One has served a prison sentence for drug-related offences.

Three have never voted in a general election.

Five have experienced abuse and neglect at the hands of a care giver.

Five took up full-time smoking at a young age.

Five have received state benefits.

Five have been in a dysfunctional relationship.

Five have experienced health problems associated with poor nutrition and lifestyle such as: being over- or under-weight, difficulty making positive choices in relation to nutrition or using high calorie, nutrient-void food to self-soothe.

Five have poor concentration that has impacted on their education.

Five suffer from social anxiety.

Five have experienced emotional and mental health problems that predispose them to stress.

Zero have gone to university.

Zero are on the housing ladder.

Zero have any savings.

Zero have access to a bank of Mum and Dad.

Zero are involved with an activist group.

Zero are active members of a political party.

Zero regularly visit libraries or places of cultural interest.

Zero go on foreign holidays at least once a year.

And none of us care for Radio 2, yoga or Quorn-based food products either.

It's a lot more striking when you think about it like that, isn't it? When it hits you that, beneath the specificity and uniqueness of our subjectively experienced individual lives, runs a road of pure inevitability from which we rarely diverge. This wouldn't be so startling if it applied to everyone, but poverty appears to be the definitive factor that dictates the direction of a person's life from the very day that they are born. Studies conducted found it was possible to predict the odds that a child will ascend to the middle class, simply by measuring their birthweight. Babies born of parents who live in areas of high deprivation are more likely to be of low birthweight compared to babies born of parents who live in areas of average and low deprivation: 8 per cent compared to 5–6 per cent.

There comes a point when being objective about this stuff starts to look like procrastination from acting. And it's also a bit glib when you're always being told to get over it by people who've never experienced it.

We often discuss the issue of poverty as if it's a physical thing, an entity that descends on communities at random and without warning. Like it's an autonomous being, over which we have no real control. For some, poverty is a quicksand that consumes us despite our best efforts to escape its pull. The more effort we make to get out, the further up to our necks we find ourselves. For others, it's a monster living on a distant hillside, a place where you should never go. Something you should be thankful you've never experienced.

All we can ever do, it seems, is stem the bleed as this unforgiving predator moves on to its next hapless victim. To be honest, I can understand why this kind of emotional disassociation occurs. I am guilty of it too when it comes to issues I'm not in proximity to. For example, when I see images of war or famine on television I feel an initial sense of shock or sorrow on behalf of the people suffering but those feelings of concern usually fade when I return to my own immediate concerns. I know a human life halfway around the world is of equal value to one on my own street, but it appears I am either uncaring, selfish or, at some level, my unevolved human brain is not designed to remain fully cognisant of the distant plights of others. Which is why, even though it bothers me, I can understand how people who don't live in poverty might be detached from the struggles of those who do. The social and cultural divides are often so wide that all we can do is make assumptions, drawing inaccurate conclusions about people we rarely mix with.

This disconnection, and the impact it has on our ability to think and discuss the matter, is a big part of the reason why poverty persists. Not only do we have gulfs in class to traverse, we also have divides in ideology, politics and individual and collective interests to consider. On the left, we believe poverty is a political choice, the effects of which could be alleviated if we were to redirect our collective resources to redistribute the wealth in our society. On the right, people believe that empowering the individual and the family to become prosperous, and reducing the role (and cost) of the state, is the best way to create a viable, socially cohesive society. Looming over this debate is an election cycle, mass media and a world of such unending complexity that our leaders often choose to oversimplify every aspect of our lives into soundbites that make it harder to consider the issue in anything but tribal and adversarial terms. But the fault doesn't always lie with those who remain unaware of the nuts and bolts of poverty, nor can it be pinned solely on politicians.

Being sentimental, sensationalist or melodramatic about it doesn't help either. Moral outrage creates as much confusion as it attempts to solve. And just because you identify yourself as someone who is poor or someone who is 'fighting' poverty, that should not absolve you from examining your own beliefs and assumptions about the matter as well. It's far more complex than many of us would like to believe. In fact, it often suits us to ignore this complexity in favour of clinging on to dogmas which align conveniently with our self-interest.

Sometimes we need a dramatic example to cut through the white noise and get directly to the heart of the issue. It's often the case that when confronted by the ugly truth of an issue that has been overcomplicated, simplified or sanitised for our consumption, the shock or anger at what we see can propel us into some form of action to confront it as a society. This action might involve organising to exert political pressure or pooling resources to alleviate suffering. But it might also inspire the sort of humility required to drop our defences and attempt to build a consensus around an issue that has, so far, been the source of dispute. It may help, therefore, to remain mindful of the fact that while poverty is relative, meaning it's not as bad in the UK as it is in Bolivia, one area where this relativity does not so easily apply is in the risk it presents to children.

16

Great Expectations

KIDS IN POVERTY, wherever they are, are exposed to a similar risk of harm, neglect, abuse and exploitation; child prostitutes on the streets of Athens, drug addicted street kids in South America, the institutional sexual abuse of orphans or baby refugees washing up on the beaches of Europe. Being poor increases the risks that vulnerable children face, regardless of whether they are born in the Third World or a developed economy, and the trauma they experience can significantly alter the direction of their life. Yes, it's certainly true to say that a western child has less chance of dying of hunger, dysentery or malaria than a child in Rwanda, but that is little consolation when you are being verbally abused, beaten or sexually assaulted in an alcoholic home. Unfortunately, we have yet to make the visceral connection between poverty and child abuse that would bring so many of the social problems in our society into sharper focus. We've yet to see the issue framed in such a way as to focus our minds away from the areas of disagreement and onto the central issue at hand: social deprivation is what drives child abuse.

And a big part of the reason why this cultural penny hasn't quite dropped is because of the way we currently think about and discuss the issue. We've all seen the standard image used by news and media outlets to signify child abuse. It's the child, usually between five and ten, sitting on some stairs in what appears to be the family home, their face often obscured by a visual effect or their hands. This image may be part of an advert for a charity or, increasingly, an item on the news accompanied by a presenter speaking in that 'now we're talking about child abuse' register.

Great care is taken to present the issue of child abuse in a manner that does not upset us as an audience. In fact, sometimes we are even warned to prepare ourselves for 'distressing' images in advance of them being broadcast. Most people, when faced with such a serious and sensitive topic such as child abuse or neglect, will experience a natural level of empathy for the victims and a corresponding anger and disgust for the parents or guardians of the victims.

In our hearts, we feel genuine sympathy for these kids, who didn't have much of a chance. Something must be done, we tell ourselves, before moving on to the next news item. The next news item might be about young people being unruly, engaging in various forms of criminality or nuisance behaviour. Or perhaps about the blight of violence and rise of addiction in our communities. We think to ourselves 'What is it with young people these days?' or 'What the hell's going on with their parents?' And there's a simple reason for that: these sanitised images, used to portray child abuse and neglect without upsetting us, distort the true nature of the problem. These pictures create a false impression that the victims are perpetual children, frozen in time, just waiting for us to reach into the photograph and remove them from harm. As children, they receive unlimited sympathy and compassion.

But the second these kids are legally culpable, our entire posture towards them changes. When the truth, whether we want to accept it or not, is that the neglected and abused kids, the unruly young people, the homeless, the alkies, the junkies and the lousy, irresponsible, violent parents are often the same person at different stages of their lives.

It's almost a cliché to point out the correlation between poverty and nearly every other social problem you care to mention. Not just economic hardship, but poverty of the sort that fertilises cultures of abuse. This problem transcends the left–right political paradigm and will eventually overwhelm any society that refuses to deal with it. And while it's important that we retain perspective and objectivity when trying to find solutions to these deep-seated social problems, it's also important we don't get so distant from the reality of human suffering that these issues become dinner party anecdotes, PowerPoint presentations or political footballs. This is not to say that the lives of all kids living in poverty are predetermined or that they lack agency when they become adults. Nor is it to absolve people of responsibility for their actions. It's simply to say that it is impractical to kick this can any further down the political road, and that we must take our fingers out of our ears and start listening to each other. Because, when these family problems do flare up, they are rarely self-contained within a household or a community.

Instead, they spill out into our society and multiply at a massive cost to all of us.

They spill into overcrowded casualty and high-dependency hospital wards. They spill into six-month-long waiting lists to access clinical psychologists and psychiatric counselling facilities. They spill into overrun social work departments and inundated supported accommodation projects barely keeping their heads above water. They spill into stressful housing offices, packed-to-capacity crisis centres and outmoded addictions services. And, for some, they spill into police stations, sheriff courts, children's homes, secure units, young offender institutions and prisons.

A vulnerable family living in constant economic uncertainty, job insecurity or subject to an inhumane sanctions regime often lacks the capacity to absorb, process and practically address life's unpredictable adversities. So much of the system is presided over by people who only understand poverty in the simplest of terms, and therefore it also reflects everything they misunderstand too. Take the UK welfare system at present, where it appears that humiliation is being used to incentivise people into finding a job. Such an approach could only be dreamt up by people who have no idea of what being born poor is really like. What it does to your mind, body and spirit. Poverty is not only about a lack of employment, but about having no margin for error while living in constant stress and unpredictability. And for children growing up in this chaos, the experience can leave them emotionally disfigured, at odds with everything around them.

A stock image of a child sitting on a step, with their head in their hands, does not adequately express this complexity; it dangerously undermines it. The over-simplified way this issue, and many others, are framed and discussed creates a false impression in the public mind of what is really driving child abuse and neglect. And, in turn, what is driving many of our current social problems where crime, violence, homelessness and addiction are concerned.

It all begins with a child living in social deprivation. When it comes to child abuse, poverty is the factory floor.

17

Children of the Dead End

MY MOTHER FANCIED herself a bit of an arsonist. On more than one occasion, I faintly recall people being preoccupied by something that mysteriously caught fire. Once I heard about a blaze through my granny, who received a phone call informing her about it; another time I was fleeing the scene myself. My mother either had a fascination with fire or fire had some sort of score to settle with her; the two crossed paths far too many times for it to be coincidental. This gave weekends at her flat in the high-rise yet another unsettling edge.

One Saturday afternoon I was down at the swing park, playing. The park was situated between the two high flats of Stirlingfauld Place and Court. Despite being very badly vandalised, the park was still of moderate quality, featuring a large and complex climbing frame, a swirling chute and a fox-slide. When visiting my mum, I spent most of my time entertaining myself and the park at the foot of the building was a reasonably safe place to do that.

I was attempting to climb up the chute with the intention of sliding back down it again. It was a manoeuvre I had performed many times without event. However, I made the mistake of climbing up as someone else was sliding down and we collided about half way up the chute. The heel of his boot tore the nail on my thumb back through my finger, creating an unsightly wound and an awful lot of blood.

Like any child that age, I started screaming for my mum. But in this kind of environment, when you call for help, it doesn't always come.

I walked around the local vicinity in agony, tears streaming down my face, trying to find her, to no avail. I couldn't access her flat either and had no idea whether she was in, and simply unconscious, or if she had gone out to get drunk at someone else's house.

Eventually, I tracked her down to the building opposite, where she was drinking with an old man in a flat not dissimilar to her own – dirty and dark. I showed her my injury. She didn't react. Perhaps it was because she was drunk or maybe she didn't think it was that bad. After all, she'd lost half a finger after attempting to gain access to her home as a child, only for a window to be mysteriously slammed down on her hands as she climbed in.

When confronted by my injury she simply told me to phone my dad, and kept on drinking.

Regardless of how frightening or dangerous life around my mother could get, it all felt strangely normal at the time.

When I was huddled with my brothers and sisters in a dark room in the middle of the night, while a man screamed death threats through the letter-box, it was scary but not unusual. When I had to run out and phone an ambulance after walking into the house to find her on the toilet having a gastric haemorrhage, it was startling but not unusual. Whether it was a child being tied to a chair for being cheeky or a baby being booted across the floor for crying by the faceless male drunk she had in occasionally, it all felt bizarrely normal. Not even the sight of her having sex was enough to shock me.

In 'deprived' areas, where resources are scarce, gossip is a form of currency and if you're unlucky enough to hail from a visibly troubled family, you are presented with a choice: you can let other people talk about it or you can become the author of your own story – which is exactly what I did.

With the dysfunction finding ever more obvious expression in my life and with no ability to keep it private, I underwent an adaptation that would change the course of my life: I began to embrace the dysfunction and used it as form of creative and social propulsion. Rather than being on the receiving end of cruel jokes about my mother, I began to hold court in school playgrounds and crack them myself. Instead of leaving it to the bullies to make light of the clouds that hung over my head, I beat them to it – and even started preparing jokes about the bullies' mums too. This became a way to accept and process trauma. Being open about my difficulties helped me to take some ownership of my life.

As I got a little older and new issues surfaced, I began to understand some of the constituent parts of the problem my family faced, whether alcoholism, violence, lifestyle or drug addiction. By the time my mother left and my sister returned from the Gorbals, a shell of her former self, the painful events that I had witnessed or experienced were becoming a form of fuel that fed a growing obsession to write. I would rush home from school to get to work on whatever project I was developing and immerse myself in these words; purging myself of trauma by vomiting everything up for anyone who would listen.

Over time, I started to see my personal experience in the wider context of a family and our home in the broader context of a community. Every few months, the scale of what I could comprehend seemed to expand and into that broadening horizon poured new possibilities to explore. Now in my teens and certain I knew everything, I started to find a small audience for my stories. The validation I got when I performed relieved many of my other anxieties. The rush and sense of self-worth gave me a deep feeling of connection to other people and the present moment where dread about the future and obsession about the past did not trouble me.

As I gained more experience, writing, speaking and perform-ing, my stories took more sophisticated forms. Then I'd learn something new that recontextualised my journey. Working on material became an obsession; no matter what I was doing, I was always in a rush to get back to my work.

After a while I popped up on the radar of some of the local organisations that were set up to 'engage' young people like me. I seemed to tick all their boxes. More and more people were on hand, offering me a platform to tell my story. The bigger the platform I got, the more people in the community seemed to connect with it. Sharing my experiences was cathartic but was also becoming a form of currency I could trade locally. Out of nothing, I suddenly had something of value. It wasn't long until I was invited back to the West End to offer my thoughts and opinions on the topic of poverty.

18

The Stranger

MY FIRST APPEARANCE on the BBC took place at my auntie's flat in Govanhill, on Glasgow's southside, where she lived with my two cousins and a mother and child she had taken in who were fighting deportation. Having got involved in the Pollok Free State, she later became a local environmental activist and was eventually elected to the Scottish Parliament as an MSP. By this point I was about to leave secondary school but had trouble getting work. I had been working as a temp in Next but was not offered a contract after the Christmas period. There was speculation that certain employers were screening potential employees based on their postcode – which was an indicator of social class. BBC Radio Scotland was covering it on the news and I was asked to come on and talk about it. It went well and I was asked back more over the course of the year.

Charities, arts organisations, youth workers and even politicians were becoming familiar with me. At events like gala days or fetes, I would be presented as an example of a young person who was doing something positive with his life. I'd be allotted time to perform or speak about my experiences and this was becoming a regular fixture of my life, even after I became homeless.

The BBC, after letting me host their flagship news programme as a guest presenter, asked me to present a four-part series called *Neds*. In Scotland, a 'ned' is like a 'chav'; a poor person, usually young, who causes disruption in their community through anti-social behaviour – which was high on the news agenda at the time. Now working at the BBC, my life represented something of a schism: on one hand I was homeless and developing a dependency on alcohol and drugs and had no self-esteem, but on the other hand I was about to become a radio presenter who travelled the country like a proper journalist. When you have no real sense of self to anchor you to reality then you become whatever the world decides you are that day. Some days I was flying high, thinking I was on my way to some kind of job and would make my family proud. Other days I was unable to get to the BBC on time because I was so hungover and depressed.

When the series ended, another was commissioned, this time a three-part show about Shettleston, a housing scheme which had among the worst health statistics in the country. I had a growing public profile and was involved with several organisations as a volunteer while making a name for myself as a local rap artist. But whether it was low self-esteem, imposter syndrome or just a self-sabotage instinct, I began to question people's motives for wanting to help me. Beneath everything, all I was looking for was connection; to feel understood, heard and supported. To feel respected, safe and loved. The praise and platforms I received certainly made me feel I was heading in the right direction, but once the novelty wore off and I began to consider what was going on more deeply, some things started bothering me. The big contradiction of my life at this point was that the people who apparently wanted to help me, with whom I craved a connection, were all being paid to be there. So it wasn't that big a leap to assume that if they weren't getting paid then they'd be away doing something else.

I also noticed that while people were always keen that I tell my story, in whichever form it took, they seemed to prefer that I stick to certain parts of it. The testimony about my childhood was fine but they were less keen on the observations I started to make as my understanding of poverty, its causes and impacts, deepened. I was growing and learning and evolving, as I had been all my life, and this created new lines of inquiry that I would immediately pursue, no matter the consequences. Queries such as 'Who makes the decisions about your budget?' and 'How do we solve poverty if all your jobs depend on it?' were making people around me nervous.

This sort of sentiment didn't seem as popular among the various youth workers, charities and journalists as the story about my dead mum. When I realised this, I soon learned to use that story as a Trojan horse, mainly because without it, people seemed much less interested in anything I had to say. It was as if the only thing that qualified my opinion was the fact I had been poor. The second I wandered off that topic people started shuffling their papers and things got awkward. It seemed my criticism was often deemed not to be constructive enough. Despite the constant talk of empowerment and giving voice to the voiceless, it was obvious many of these people were only interested in my thoughts if they were about my experience as a 'poor' person. It was assumed that people like me had very little insight on anything else. This was disheartening and confusing. I couldn't figure out if people wanted to associate with me because I was smart or because they wanted to use me in some way. Having very little self-esteem, it led to wild fluctuations in my sense of who I was. Sometimes I felt my ideas were of value, other times I was crushed by the terrible thought that I had just been kidding myself. That I was worthless and stupid. But rather than buckle beneath that confusion it seemed to stoke the flames of my anger. The conflict seemed to concentrate my mind, just like fear, and the things that upset me, just like traumatic experiences, became a form of fuel.

Even mental illness and problems in my personal life didn't stop me from pursuing my lines of inquiry and going after my targets. I followed my instincts, right or wrong, despite the fact I could sense resistance to the message I was transmitting. Eventually, like the books and poems teachers tried to make me read, I began to take an adversarial attitude towards the people and organisations I believed were trying to influence how I thought and spoke about these issues. I began to lash back against anybody I felt was manipulating me, either to pacify my criticism or to extract narrative or data for their own agendas.

My story, which I had been conditioned to retell like a party piece, got me so far and then people became wary of me, aggravating my sense of rejection and exclusion. I was learning that there were limits to what you could say when you wanted to talk about poverty. I was learning that even the harshest childhood experience wouldn't get you a free pass to cast a critical eye on the structures around you. But I was also learning that the emotional damage that growing up in poverty had done to me, made it that much harder for me to engage with the very people deployed to help me. I often projected my pain, mistrust and sense of exclusion onto people who really did mean well. I was never quite sure if my instincts were right or if I was in the grip of an episode of mania.

What I soon learned was that, no matter your background, you are cast out the second you offend the people who're in charge of your empowerment. Sometimes it's a person, other times it's an organisation. Sometimes it's a movement and other times it's a political party. But the minute you start telling your story in service of your own agenda and not theirs, you're discarded. Your criticism is dismissed as not being constructive. Your anger is attributed to your mental health problems and everything about you that people once applauded becomes a stick they beat you with. Look out for these people. The people who pay wonderful lip service to giving the working class a voice, but who start to look very nervous whenever we open our mouths to speak.

I never regarded my childhood as hard until I saw the look on people's faces when I talked about it. I never assumed that my life, or indeed I, was interesting or significant in any way until people started telling me so. I never assumed I had anything of value to say until people began prompting me to repeat this poverty narrative over and over. But if I happened to stray off script, then curtains would mysteriously close, lights would mysteriously fade, microphones would mysteriously cut out. The BBC didn't offer me any more work. The anti-social behaviour news agenda had moved on. They didn't even respond to my pitch about another programme. The week the *Neds* series came out, the *Sunday Mail*, who had interviewed me earlier in the week and sent a photographer out to take pictures to promote the show, ran a story called 'Neddy Burns'. In it they used a picture of me in which my hat had been blown up by the wind, appearing to sit at the same angle as the stereotypical 'chav'. The minute the social deprivation agenda dried up in the media, there was no longer any need for me. I thought I had been asked to take part because people valued my insight. Because I had something to say. Then one day it dawned on me why they had asked me to present *Neds* in the first place: it was because they thought I was a ned.

Today I know better. Today I understand that my poverty narrative is viewed by many as an opportunity, as opposed to something with inherent value that people who read books could learn from. Please understand that I think no less of those who inadvertently helped create that impression, nor do I think for one moment that people employed in the poverty industry have anything but good intentions. The issue here was my assumption. Perhaps due to my radical roots in far-left communities and may-be my naivety as a young person, I always just thought the aim was to dismantle poverty. However, once you see the mechanics of the poverty industry up close, you realise it's in a state of per-manent growth and that without individuals, families and com-munities in crisis there would no longer be a role for these massive institutions.

I've been wheeled out by organisations and political groups and had my 'powerful', 'honest', 'heart-breaking' testimony offered as proof of the changes we need to make as a society when it comes to poverty. But the moment my lines of enquiry change, relative to my growth, understanding or aspiration, and my critical eye turns to those who would repurpose my story for their own agendas, whether it be an activist, a charity or a politician, then I am cast out as an 'arrogant', 'aggressive', 'dangerous', 'self-sorry', 'indulgent', 'ego-maniacal' 'pseudo-intellectual lightweight' 'sell-out' 'who always makes everything about him'. All fair criticisms. I am certainly not a flawless person. But all I've ever done is talk about poverty. And the only way anyone would listen to what I had to say was if I prefaced my opinion with personal testimony about my dead, alcoholic mother and what a difficult childhood I had. I don't write about myself because I think I'm important, it's because that's what I've been conditioned to do in order to be heard. That's the sort of window dressing that is required before the great and the good become willing to take lower class people seriously.

Even at 33 years old, this theme continues to define my life. Well I've told you all about my life, now here's what I would really like to say.

I no longer believe poverty is an issue our politicians can solve. Not because they don't want to, but because an honest conversation about what it will require is too politically difficult to have. If those in power were straight about what addressing this problem would require it would shock us to our core. And not merely because of the magnitude of the task facing society, which is unconscionable in scale, but also because there is a certain level of personal responsibility involved that's become taboo to acknowledge on the left. For all the demand we in left-wing circles feign for fundamental change and radical action, people get a bit touchy and offended when you suggest that might apply to them too. The truth, whether we want to accept it or not, is that when it comes to poverty – not as a political football but as a global phenomenon in which we all play an active role – there is no one actor or group that we can blame with any certainty.

Contrary to what we've been told, the issue of poverty is far too complex to blame solely on 'Tories' or 'elites'. It's precisely because of the complexity at play, and how difficult it is to grasp, that we look for easy scapegoats. Whether it be the left blaming the rich or the right blaming the poor, we tend only to be interested in whichever half of the story absolves us of responsibility for the problem. That's not the sort of thing a politician looking to get elected can say to a potential voter.

Poverty has become a game played between a few competing political teams. The teams vary from country to country but the rules of the game are usually the same. Blame for poverty is always ascribed to someone else; an outgroup that we are told not only enables poverty and benefits from it, but also gets a kick out of people being poor. This game is so underhanded and cynical that the truth, itself, only becomes true when it can be appropriated, weaponised and redeployed by one side against the others. Rather than admit that nobody really knows what to do, besides tweak some knobs here and there, our hapless leaders, with their own immediate political dilemmas to consider, simply pretend to have the situation under control. And when they inevitably break their empty promises, made in haste to placate our anger, they tell us it's because the other teams are deliberately impeding progress. This game is played by all parties, regardless of which end of the spectrum they claim. And we eat this nonsense up like f***ing children.

Let's take a moment to truly consider the damage this game is doing to our society.

When one political party blames another for the problem, it creates a false impression in the public mind that this complex issue is within the competence of one political actor or group to solve. This is a dangerous oversimplification. An oversimplification which forces us to cast one another as heroes and villains in the long-running saga of poverty, often based on our unconscious bias, false beliefs and, increasingly, our resentments. Just like stress creates a demand for relief through alcohol, food and drugs, so too does our refusal to get serious about grappling with the complexity of poverty; creating a demand for the sort of political juvenilia that reduces every person to a caricature and every issue to a soundbite. These partisan rivalries are now so toxic that the idea of getting around a table with your opponents, in good faith, is almost laughable. Proposing such an idea is regarded widely as naive. Meanwhile, trying to build a consensus or, God forbid, acknowledging the virtue or integrity of people you disagree with politically or conceding where other ideas have succeeded, can get you publicly shamed and lynched – by your own team.

Not even the stark reality of child abuse, the inexorable rise of crime, the ubiquity of violence, the horror of domestic abuse, the scourge of homelessness or the tragic inevitability of alcoholism or addiction that underscores so much of it is enough to humble us into showing some contrition in the face of this issue. This despite knowing fine well that we'll never be able to address a problem of this scale in any meaningful way without input from right across the political spectrum. We'd rather play games. Sadly, there is absolutely no incentive whatsoever for a politician to be honest about the true extent of this problem. Let's be honest, we wouldn't accept it. We all need someone to blame. For some it's the bankers and for others it's the poor themselves. We've become so tribal in our thinking that politicians have little choice but to supply our demand for illusory quick fixes, over-simplified soundbites, scapegoats and comforting, reassuring platitudes that conveniently ascribe blame to the people we don't like. It's a truly sorry state and if blame is being apportioned, there's certainly enough to go around every one of us.

In these conditions of tribalism, bad faith and political uncertainty, the problem is only likely to get worse. The time has come to face this reality which will place a heavy burden on those of us who are resolved to see progress on this matter. With no appetite for cross-party consensus and even less for radical change, despite the odd flourish of rebellion every few years, people with an interest in helping the poor (or themselves for that matter) must now begin grappling with the notion that this system, and all its internal contradiction, is here to stay for the foreseeable future – certainly for the lifetime of anyone reading this book in the year 2017.

And while insurgent political parties and social movements may force grudging concessions from the powerful, much as they did throughout the last century on a range of issues, the sort of fundamental shift required to truly tackle poverty at the root is unlikely to materialise within our lifetimes. That doesn't mean people should stop fighting for what they believe in. Nor does it mean we should submit to forces that are clearly acting against our interests. Just that we should let go of the idea that all we require is for capitalism to collapse or for a new country to be created and everything will just work itself out. It won't.

The only thing worse than an unjust economic system is an unjust economic system when it implodes. The idea of rubbing our hands waiting for this to happen is, at best, exceptionally uninspiring. At worst, it's short-sighted and slightly sinister. Once we accept this is wishful thinking, we can channel our energy in other directions based on a more realistic assessment of what is currently possible. As well as discussing and debating the abstracts of 'the system' we can also begin considering less intangible aspects of poverty that are within our immediate grasp to address. As I've already outlined, poverty comprises many domains of the human experience: social, psychological, emotional, political and cultural. Some things we can't immediately impact, like the economy. Others we can affect intermittently, like political parties. But other areas, such as our mental health, consumer behaviour or lifestyle, which also play a significant role in our quality of life, are not as intangible and inalterable. What we now need to ask ourselves, as a matter of urgency, is which aspects of poverty can we positively affect through our own thinking and action? If poverty is negatively affecting our quality of life, is there any action we could take to mitigate this harm? Ultimately, which aspects of poverty are beyond our control and which are within our capability to change?

On the left, I see constant talk of new economic systems, of overthrowing elites or of increasing public spending. I see endless debate about the overlapping, interdependent structural oppressions of western society and the symbolic violence inherent in capitalism. But I rarely see anyone talking about emotional literacy. It's rare to see a debate about over-eating. I never see activists being more open about their drink problems and drug habits or the psychological problems fuelling them.

Nobody ever seems to be writing a dissertation on the link between emotional stress and chronic illness or writing an op-ed about how they managed to give up smoking. As if somehow, these day-to-day problems are less consequential to the poor than the musings of Karl Marx. As if somehow, we can postpone action on the things that are demoralising, incapacitating and killing us until after the hypothetical revolution. Beneath all the theoretical discussion and torturous terminology about politics and economics, these problems of mind, body and spirit and what we do to manage them as individuals, families and communities, are the unglamorous, cyclical dilemmas that many people are really struggling with.

These are the issues that compound poverty-related stress. These are the problems that make people apathetic, depressed, confrontational, chronically ill and deeply unhappy. And it's these painful emotions that drive much of the self-defeating consumer behaviour that delivers adrenalin to the heart of the very economic system many on the left allegedly want to dismantle. Yet on these matters we, on the left, have very little to say. Or at least, very little that people in deprived communities are interested in listening to. And it's not hard to understand why.

Every problem is discussed like it's beyond the expertise of the average person. The cumulative effect being that responsibility for poverty and its attendant challenges is almost always externalised; ascribed to an unseen force or structure, a system or some vaguely defined elite. These things are undoubtedly constituent parts of the problem, but our analysis rarely acknowledges the complexity of poverty as it is experienced by human beings, day-to-day. A systemic analysis which focuses on external factors unwisely foregoes the opportunity to explore the role we, as individuals, families and communities, can play in shaping the circumstances that define our lives. A systemic analysis does not account for the subtleties of poverty at ground level; the link between false belief and self-defeating action that keeps so many of us trapped in a spin cycle of stress and thoughtless consumption.

But these problems, as banal as they seem, are as fundamental to tackling poverty at the root as any critique of an economic system. Yet, rather than integrate this truth into our analysis, we have allowed right wing movements to monopolise the concept of personal agency and the notion of taking responsibility. Worse, we vilify anybody who implies that poor people may sometimes play a role in their own circumstances, whether they be desirable or adverse. We've forgotten that not every problem or issue can be ascribed to broader social problem or power dynamic. We deny the objective truth that many people will only recover from their mental health problems, physical illnesses and addictions when they, along with the correct support, accept a certain level of culpability for the choices they make. Yet such an assertion has become offensive to our ears despite being undeniably true. When was the last time you heard a prominent left-wing figure speak of the power inherent within each of us to overcome adversity and transform the conditions of our own lives?

I'll wait.

Instead, we peddle the naive idea that everything will be fine just as soon as the current system breaks down. We push the lie that trading one political or economic system for another is merely a painless formality. We set forth the proposition that it's easier to redesign an entire society to suit our ever-evolving personal needs than it is to make some moderate adjustments to our own thinking and behaviour. And we cry foul any time somebody in our own ranks has the temerity to point this stuff out. So, I apologise if you think this isn't constructive. In the absence of real leadership, it's time we demanded more of ourselves. Not because it's easy or fair but because we have no other choice. We must now evolve beyond our dependence on political figures to map out reality on our behalf. Poverty is not a game and it's going nowhere any time soon. Poverty is here to stay and things will get worse before they improve. That's the truth our leaders know but don't have the guts to tell us.

Which is why we must open another frontier in politics. Not one solely based on railing against the system, but also about scrutinising our own thinking and behaviour. One which is about reclaiming the idea of personal responsibility from a rampant and socially misguided right wing that has come to monopolise it. A new leftism which is not only about advocating radical change but also about learning to take ownership of as many of our problems as we can so that we may begin rebuilding the depleted human capacity in our poorest communities.

In this far bleaker context, where politicians have no real solutions and can't even bring themselves to discuss the matter honest-

ly, what hope can we offer to people living their lives right now – without filling their heads with false hope or lies? What do we have to say to the people who won't be around when the third industrial revolution begins? The people who'll never see Universal Basic Income being rolled out? Well, I suppose we could start by being honest: There will be no revolution. Not in your lifetime. This system will limp on and so must we.

Much of the reason this system endures is directly related to how we think, feel and behave as individuals, families and communities. Just as we are products of our environment, our environments are also a product of us. From the foods we consume, to the products we buy. The newspapers we read to the politicians we vote for. So many of the problems we face, that we often attribute to 'the system' are, to some extent, self-generated. Therefore, many of these problems (though certainly not all) are within our individual and collective competence to positively affect. Considering this, and in the absence of a bloodless revolt any time soon, the question for people on the left is no longer simply 'how do we radically transform the system', but also, 'how do we radically transform ourselves?'

And something about my dead mum.

19

Tales From the Mall

TODAY I STAND defeated at the counter of a McDonald's, where I appear to be ordering food against my will. I'm now entering my third week of eating junk food, having previously managed to lose ten pounds during a period of abstinence. This success makes my regression into emotional eating more difficult to stomach. I know this feeling well. After all, it's not the first time I've relapsed.

I take the food to my table, mortified that I might be seen by someone I know. I tell myself, this is the last time. In my head, I continually perform calculations that involve calories, kilograms, litres, pounds. Running parallel to these estimations I tally up miles, kilometres and steps. My apps track everything I eat and drink, every act of physical exertion. Throughout the day I receive a constant stream of data. But if knowledge is power, why do I feel so pathetic and weak? So overweight?

All bad habits involve a routine, any deviation from which creates anxiety and agitation. This stress triggers the urge to resume the habitual behaviour, a powerful impulse that can override all other considerations.

In other words, when my brain wants a McDonald's and I'm tired or stressed, then the urge is very hard to disobey. I open the box containing the chicken burger and empty a portion of fries into the lid, laid out flat like a little cardboard bowl. I start with a couple of stray fries that have fallen onto the table and then turn my attention to the straw, tearing the wrapper and unsheathing it with my teeth. The straw is then placed in the large plastic cup and I take my first sip of Coca Cola.

The ice-cold fizzy drink rejuvenates me and I am filled with a wave of optimism bordering on elation. The shame is banished from my mind. But I immediately squander this wave of positivity by fantasising about a life where I never visit McDonald's again.

I return to the fries. This time a bigger handful is required, followed by a swig of Coke. The process of eating and drinking accelerates and my appetite gets more ferocious as more food enters my system. Which is why I have taken my usual precaution of ordering an extra portion of fries. It's always comforting to know it's there, almost like the company of another person, but without the social anxiety.

The quantity of food I can consume in this gluttonous trance is obscene. Scrolling through my phone, reading people's accounts of falling off their diets, I grow increasingly disgusted at myself. It's like my brain forgets that I'm full and goes into autopilot. The rush of elation soon passes and melancholy descends. I look around. Most of the people in the restaurant are also overweight and alone. I wonder if, for them, too, the temporary high of those first delectable mouthfuls is a curtain raiser to the deep feelings of shame and powerlessness that push us through the door in the first place.

I don't think it's possible to be overweight and enjoy this food. Some people might be able to kid themselves, but I see them struggling to fit into their cars when they leave. I see them staring into space across the road from the chip shop, debating whether to put the health kick on hold. The thought of those first few bites, the emotional relief and instant fulfilment they induce, possesses such an allure that resistance is futile; an allure so intoxicating that you forget things you swore you would always remember. Like how deeply it depresses you to obsess about this sort of food and gorge on it.

Only days ago, I was hiding sweet and chocolate wrappers in a jacket pocket because I didn't want my partner to know I had been bingeing again. Yes, there are millions of people who enjoy McDonald's in moderation. But for people of my disposition, with serious impulse control problems, emotional eating is not only dangerous but also soul-destroying. The thought at the end of the meal is always the same: I don't know why I did that. This cycle of emotional discomfort and self-defeating behaviour extends to many other areas of my life. For many years, I believed my lifestyle and associated health problems – fatigue, depression, anxiety, gum disease, insomnia, toothache, obesity, sexual dysfunction, alcoholism and substance misuse – were by-products of capitalism. In many ways they are. But that's not the whole story.

Like many people my age, my terrible eating habits can be traced directly to my grandmother. She was born in the early '30s and grew up in a time when the food products we now associate with poor lifestyle either hadn't been invented or were very hard to come by. This was a time before mass public transport, mechanisation and telecommunications, which meant that people were likely to be engaged in physical work every day, probably walking to and from their jobs. Physical exercise was a constituent part of everyday life. It was in the early '30s that the first American drive-in restaurants started popping up, signalling the dawn of a new age of tasty and affordable fast food. This phenomenon, and the problems that came to be associated with it, would likely have arrived in the UK a lot sooner. We temporarily dodged that bullet by becoming engulfed in the Second World War.

By the time my grandparents met in the mid-'50s consumerism began to take hold and the processed foods of today made their appearance in local grocery shops. Imagine what this must have been like for people who had lived through wartime rationing. The impact was felt both in terms of how consumers perceived and related to food and how producers, hungry for market share, produced and packaged it. Eating was no longer simply about fuelling and nurturing your body. It was about expressing yourself and exploring new realms of personal pleasure.

By the time the UK started integrating with Europe in the '70s, the food revolution was well under way. Consumers became spoiled for choice as companies competed fiercely for their custom. Links were identified between processed foods and health problems such as high cholesterol. With growing public awareness of these risks, a sub-industry grew offering low-fat, seemingly healthy, alternatives. Before long, healthy eating became bamboozling and counterintuitive, a minefield to traverse.

The concept of food, how it should be sourced, produced and eaten, changed more in my grandparents' lifetime than at any other period in human history. Yet, our understanding of what was really going on in our food and, indeed, nutrition generally remained dangerously unevolved. And by the time we had educated ourselves, it was already too late – we were a family of sugar addicts.

My journey into eating poorly started early in life, hastened by the fact that we were unaware of the dangers. As kids, we'd queue up outside the dinner hall in school, talking about what we were going to have for lunch that day. To call it a preoccupation would be an understatement. Salty soup, pies, pastries, chips, roast potatoes, battered fish, sausages and breaded chicken, covered in baked beans, mushy peas and fatty gravy. Desserts were obligatory, consisting of caramel cakes, empire biscuits, Angel Delight, jelly or a choc-ice – all available with custard. Before lunchtime a tuck-trolley would roll through our classrooms, interrupting lessons for up to 15 minutes, filled to the brim with chocolate bars, chewy sweets, fizzy drinks, fruit juices and crisps.

Obtaining and consuming these 'treats' became a central occupation that made playtime as much about sweets as it was about play. I began making emotional associations with certain kinds of food, which soon evolved into an expectation of entitlement to sweets at specific times. If this expectation was not met or there was an interruption to the flow of sugar, then I'd experience anger, frustration and disappointment. This preoccupation led to dips in energy throughout the day and affected my ability to concentrate. If I found myself without tuck because I didn't get any pocket money, playtime was tinged with melancholy. Days were longer if I didn't have treats to look forward. My love for sweets was so deep that threatening to withhold them from me was – excluding violence – about the only way to control my behaviour.

Luckily, at my grandparents' there was rarely a disruption in supply.

Much of my childhood was spent on the other side of Pollok, with my granny. She performed the dual role of mother and grandmother. We spent a lot of time 'going for a loaf', as she called it. 'Going for a loaf' was code for a day trip. Codes were important because they helped us communicate without drawing the suspicion or interference of my grandfather.

My granny and I spent quite a lot of time in classic Scottish cafés. The main ingredients of those Scottish cafés were Italian proprietors, some frying pans and copious amounts of American and English food. The thing that made them 'Scottish' was the fact that you could have ice cream, Turkish Delight and cigarettes between courses.

The first thing you are likely to see when you enter one of these cafés today is a fridge full of brightly coloured fizzy drinks, cans and bottles. You will often experience a cramped sensation, as too many objects are occupying too little space. Despite that, the café retains its frothy charm, though upon closer inspection its allure gets harder to put your finger on. As you squeeze through the clutter towards the only seat available, you might become aware that the place is quite dirty. The red leather seats are not particularly comfortable either. The wooden tables, normally fixed to the floor, impose on your already receding space. More so if you have a belly – which everyone in here does.

The menu, usually wedged in a plastic holder between some weathered looking condiments, is very basic, consisting mainly of different combinations of chips, sausages, eggs and beans. Scottish working class cuisine is, essentially, a children's menu, but served in adult portions. Then, when the food is served, usually a little too quickly, it suddenly dawns on you why you remained here, despite all the signs that you might be safer eating somewhere else: the room is encased within four walls of pure sugar. Jars of brightly coloured sweets, chocolate and chews, coming in every shape and size, adorn the walls around you.

As you horse down your deep-fried dinner, you ponder your surroundings.

Is this a sweet shop? Is it a restaurant? Is it a newsagent or perhaps an ice cream van stuck in a thicket?

Nobody knows. And in Scotland, nobody cares. Even the middle class is in on it, just so long as the food is served with a dollop of irony.

At my gran's, if eating out wasn't on the menu, there was plenty of food in the house. We usually started the day with a heaped bowl of Sugar Puffs or cornflakes, glazed with a tablespoon or two of sugar, drowned in ice-cold 'blue milk' – full fat milk, signified by a blue lid. My gran did not believe in low fat products and thought them tasteless and packed full of junk. Nothing drew her formidable ire more than a margarine enthusiast or someone lecturing her about the danger of cheese. Throughout the afternoon, we would snack on white bread caked in thick butter and large mugs of tea with two or three sugars, nibbling on biscuits intermittently. We would even drink Carnation milk directly from the tin if conventional treats were in short supply. I remember placing a teaspoon on top of an open can of condensed milk and counting how long it took to fully submerge in the thick yellow liquid, before dribbling it slowly down my throat.

The ubiquity of sugar in my childhood is typified by my first Halloween. I went from door to door, dressed as can of Coca-Cola, begging neighbours for chocolate.

Evidently, while the system plays a significant role in how we choose to live our lives, we cannot underestimate the role our choices also play. And never before have we had so many things to choose from.

Clearly, capitalism is a major factor in determining matters of lifestyle, health and self-image. It can be hard to see how best to lead an ethical, environmentally friendly life while setting a good example for our children. Many of us see capitalism as the impediment to these aspirations – and with good reason.

But what about all the cheap 24-hour gyms in my area?

Or the fresh, organic, locally sourced produce I can get delivered to my door?

Then there are resources like YouTube, where I can literally learn anything I desire about food, whether it be tips on how to lose weight or advice on how to prepare healthy meals cheaply in as little time as possible.

Aren't these things also available because of capitalism?

And as a leftie, is it taboo to acknowledge this?

20

A Disaffection

POVERTY IS ABOUT more than money. Hopefully, I've convinced you of that by now if you weren't already. Poverty is more like a gravitational field comprising social, economic, emotional, physiological, political and cultural forces. Each person's escape velocity is different, relative to their specific circumstance. But, regardless of how those individual factors, such as family or education, differ between individuals, poverty and the forces it brings to bear are likely to determine the course of a person's life. That's why we can accurately predict a child's social mobility and life expectancy based solely on their birthweight, where they were born and the social class of their parents. It's why we see certain behaviours, like violence, and health problems, like obesity, that appear to affect the poor disproportionately, indicating poverty may be a proximate cause. The fact there is disparity between the social classes is undeniable; the disagreement is about how that inequality should be addressed and who is, ultimately, responsible for evening the odds.

Some believe poverty is the result of an unjust system. Others believe the system performs well and that people who cannot overcome their difficulties must take more personal responsibility. Whatever the truth, the conversation about poverty is, itself, an unfortunate by-product of the very inequality at the root of the issue. This is because the conversation about poverty is usually dominated by people with little direct experience of being poor. This conversation takes place in a cultural domain comprising of news, the arts, aspects of the public, private and third sectors and academia, and shapes how we think about and subsequently discuss poverty. From this realm, the main tenets of the debate around the issue are set and then subsequently framed for our consumption. Much like the issue of child abuse, in the context of social deprivation, those who shape the discussion about poverty often lack the necessary insight to accurately represent the issue. This creates a gulf between the people who want to sort it and the people who experience it.

It's this deficit, between those who tend to lead the conversation and those who experience the issue, that not only impedes progress, but also leads to people in poverty feeling misrepresented or excluded by 'culture'.

Culture is a very broad term that can mean many things. Your knife and fork is culture. It's how we dress, what we do in our spare time and how we talk to each other. It's what we believe, who we sleep with and why we disagree with other people on certain issues. But as well as all that, culture is also a commodity; an experience, curated for us, into which we can become invested. Terms like 'mainstream culture' or 'popular culture' attempt to describe what the average person likes. Everything else is a 'sub-culture'. However, despite there being more culture to consume than ever before, as well as more points of access in terms of participating as both consumers and creators, many people still feel misrepresented or excluded.

For example, women, the LGBTQI community, ethnic and religious minorities and the disabled have fought for decades to be fairly represented and portrayed in education, the arts and the media. They fought for fairer representation because when they engaged with the 'mainstream culture' they never saw themselves adequately reflected, or if they did they were often presented as a caricature based on someone else's privileged assumption. Increasingly, these conversations about cultural exclusion are drawn along lines of identity. Identity, our sense of who we are and our personal relationship with culture, has become one of the biggest factors in why some feel marginalised. But much like poverty, everyone's interpretation of identity is different. Two people could be objectively identical in terms of their ethnicity, nationality, religion, gender and sexuality, but may not see themselves as similar at all. They may even feel offended at the suggestion, because they identify with completely different things. This makes it a little tricky for people who create culture, because they must keep up with our ever evolving sense of ourselves – or risk being accused of excluding people.

In Scotland, there are some people who identify as Scottish and some who see themselves as British. Those who feel Scottish will often draw a clear distinction between their concept of Scottish culture and what they regard as the dominant British culture, many believing one takes precedence over the other. For example, some people in Scotland feel aggrieved about the fact we don't have our own six o'clock news programme. Instead, the news is beamed in from London. Others believe the angle the UK is shown at on screen during weather forecasts is a deliberate attempt to obscure Scotland's true geographical size in relation to England. Some believe this is done to reinforce England as the dominant culture, that Scotland is regarded as a region of England, as opposed to a country, and is therefore underrepresented or unfairly stereotyped. But there are many in Scotland for whom nationality is not the primary factor of their identity and who therefore do not see culture through that lens. For some, it's gender or race. For others, it's religious or political beliefs. The point is, people tend to assess culture based on their own individual sense of who they are. Identity becomes the lens through which everything is viewed.

It's usually the case that those who feel misrepresented or marginalised by an aspect of mainstream culture attribute this misrepresentation to either the ignorance or malign intentions of a more dominant, privileged class. For some people it's men, for some it's white people, for some it's able-bodied or straight people and for others it's the English or the Americans. Everyone sees the world through their own particular lens, so it will not surprise you, given the subjective nature of culture and identity, that I am going to make the argument that class, above all, remains the primary dividing line in our society. In truth, it's less a line and more an industrial-scale wound. Whether placing your blind faith in the advice of a doctor, being assessed or disciplined by a teacher, interviewed by a social worker or children's panel, cuffed by a police officer and advised by a lawyer before appearing in front of a judge, class is the elephant in every room.

It's no great surprise that when lower class people interface with a mainstream culture, created predominantly by and for people from higher up the food chain, whether it be newspapers, television or radio, that they often feel they're viewing a parody of reality. The reality with which they are presented appears so jarringly disfigured that they are forced to scratch their heads and ask 'Who the hell comes up with this stuff?' The questions being posed and the issues being explored in 'mainstream culture' often feel infuriatingly shallow, twee or wide-of-the-mark. This is nobody's fault, but too often culture itself becomes something people feel they exist outside of.

However, contrary to the conspiracy theories many of us concoct to explain it, there may be a far simpler explanation for why mainstream culture leaves so many noses out of joint: social mobility. The concerns of the dominant social classes become more culturally prominent than others because the dominant classes are more socially mobile. It follows that they would ascend to positions of influence and preside over a society that reflects their own interests. If you come from a more affluent background and are more socially mobile, then it's comparatively easier for you to move up the ladder and maintain your position because you have less distance to travel and aren't carrying as much baggage. This explains why, those who begin life farther up the food chain tend to end up either owning, managing, prescribing, running, directing, publishing, commissioning, editing, administering or legislating for every aspect of our lives. Even organisations that appear to care about the needs and concerns of the lower classes, like charities or tabloid newspapers, are usually controlled by people who have only a theoretical conception of what being poor entails. There are, of course, exceptions to the rule but the further up you go, the more aware you become of a prevailing sensibility that one must not offend. One which is increasingly at odds with everyone else. This specialist class have their hands firmly on the levers at every level of society and naturally create it in their own image by doing what we all do: assuming their interests, preferences and aspirations are universal. Anything outside of that is a 'counter-culture', an insurgency or a glitch in the matrix.

You must assume that nobody wants anyone else to feel excluded. But when attempting to express our thoughts and opinions across vast gulfs in social and cultural experience, nuance gets lost in translation. Good intentions become obscured and the wider the gulf, the likelier the chance of a misunderstanding. It's this tension between the various competing perspectives that festers under the bonnet of our society, becoming an engine of resentment, bad faith and even hate. In Scotland, the poverty industry is dominated by a left-leaning, liberal, middle class. Because this specialist class is so genuinely well-intentioned when it comes to the interests of people in deprived communities, they get a bit confused, upset and offended when those very people begin expressing anger towards them. It never occurs to them, because they see themselves as the good guys, that the people they purport to serve may, in fact, perceive them as chancers, careerists or charlatans. They regard themselves as champions of the under class and therefore, should any poor folk begin to get their own ideas or, God forbid, rebel against the poverty experts, the blame is laid at the door of the complainants for misunderstanding what is going on. In fact, these types are often so certain of their own insight and virtue that they won't think twice before describing working class people they purport to represent, as engaging in self-harm if they vote for a right-wing political party. Not only does this broadcast a worrying lack of self-awareness regarding why many are turning away from the left, but it also implies that those who no longer see the value in our ideas or methods are not just ungrateful, but also stupid.

21

Garnethill

IN 2014, THE Glasgow School of Art caught fire. It was a unique building designed by Charles Rennie Macintosh and its loss was spoken of in the language of national tragedy. Pictures of the blaze adorned the front page of every paper and politicians like then First Minister Alex Salmond as well as celebrities like Brad Pitt responded almost instantly, deploying vast resources and guaranteeing financial assistance to the School and the students affected. The Art School's prominent place in our national psyche provoked such a broad public response that the incident, in which nobody died or was injured, dominated the headlines for days. But the public response wasn't that broad. In truth, it was very narrow. The reaction only came from a certain section of the public, who felt connected to the Art School in some way. Most people in Glasgow weren't that bothered. After a few days of constant talk of the fire, its implications and whether the damage was permanent or could be salvaged, some (myself included) began to get irritated by what felt like the disproportionate coverage. Many of us were offended at the amount of time dedicated to this story, not just because we had no real interest in contemporary art, but because we grew up in communities where things burn down all the time. Where schools are bulldozed against our wishes. Where cultural heritage is seized before being turned over to private developers. Where roads are built through our land so that people from the suburbs can drive to places like the Glasgow School of Art without having to wait in offensive traffic queues.

'But it's the art school,' people cried, implying their interests were universal. 'Who gives a toss?' was the uneducated, vulgar response. The perception of the Glasgow School of Art, to those who felt connected to it, was equal to the lack of concern of those who didn't. But in the days that followed, there was no scrutiny or discussion of why so many people didn't care. Apparently, that wasn't interesting or important. There was only an assumption that those who didn't partake in the national grief were uncultured. Because, you know, there could be no other explanation; no legitimate reason not to care about the Glasgow School of Art, because, you know, it's the Glasgow School of Art. Such a backward view could only be the result of a lack of understanding. But it's arguable that it was those who considered themselves educated and cultured who were missing the point.

That same summer, Glasgow was to host the Commonwealth Games. If the media and politicians were to be believed, this was a time of unbroken national unity and pride. But in the shadow of the games, residents of the surrounding schemes of Bridgeton, Parkhead and Dalmarnock were angry about the disruption to their daily lives and the lack of consultation prior to these disruptions. This received very little press attention. Granted, a couple of local newspapers did cover it, but the story got lost in the carnival narrative engulfing the country. Instead, Glasgow City Council positively beamed about the jewel in the crown of their Commonwealth extravaganza: a public Wi-Fi system, designed especially for the games so that affluent international sports fans could explore the city without having to log out of Facebook. As well as the new Wi-Fi service, thousands of signs were placed around the city, in over 50 languages, directing people to and from venues, stadia and various other places of cultural interest. Meanwhile, in historically deprived communities like Cranhill, in Glasgow's East End, which still haven't been signposted despite existing for over 60 years, community centres were providing a Wi-Fi service that would make the '90s blush. Young people, at war with exasperated community centre staff and police, were terrorising the area with acts of vandalism and arson. Bouquets of dead flowers were tied to the fence just along from a playpark, marking another senseless alcohol fuelled death. These are the type of communities where trains don't run to, where buses timetables aren't worth the paper they are printed on.

But everyone was so caught up the in the carnival narrative constructed, mainly by all the people who had been cut into the Commonwealth action, that nobody realised the shameful levels of social deprivation and political exclusion running parallel to the shindig. As Glasgow City Council and the Scottish Government basked in the glory of international recognition, poor communities were being disrupted, ignored and patronised. To add insult to injury, they were also priced out of the games as well as many of the peripheral events set up to cash in. Meanwhile, back in Cranhill, if you walked into the library, it could take as long as 15 minutes for a computer to fully boot up and become operational. Then you had the shoddy Wi-Fi service to contend with. People, sitting in their homes watching the carnival on television could have been forgiven for thinking: am I living in the same world as these people? But by expressing displeasure or frustration about the galling inequity at play, then you rain on the parade. You're seen as obstructing progress or regarded as incapable of grasping the broader picture of what is really going on. You are not being 'constructive'. When you live in these communities, it always feels as if your concerns are regarded as narrow-minded, short-sighted and parochial; the story that ascends is the story that meets the needs of the many. Which, coincidentally, usually aligns with what many in these areas would regard as 'middle class'. See Stewart Lee for an example of this.

Perhaps that could explain why some people, in the aftermath of Brexit, began referring to an 'elite intelligensia' to the absolute delight of many Stewart Lee enthusiasts. They were, perhaps clumsily, trying to describe the phenomenon whereby the accepted culture, comprising news, politics and entertainment, which they were presented with every day, was contradicted and undermined by the reality of their own lives. Perhaps they were trying to express how the vast contrast between the world they were being presented with as reality and the one they were actually living in, was so stark that they could only conclude it was a deliberate fabrication.

Granted, this conclusion is often rooted in paranoia and a lack of insight into the decision-making processes taking place inside government and the media. Lack of insight often leads to the creation of myths as people pour hyperbole into the gaps in their understanding. But these assumptions aren't always that wide of the mark. It's quite true that people who work across culture, framing, dissecting and superimposing meaning onto events, for the rest of us to consume, very often hail from more privileged backgrounds than the demographics they cater to. So naturally, it leads to a cultural narrative that leaves many people scratching their heads.

Brexit Britain, in all it's dysfunction, disorder and vulgarity, is perhaps a glimpse of what happens when people start becoming aware of the fact they haven't been cut into the action but have no real mechanism to enfranchise themselves beyond voting. Brexit Britain is a snapshot of how things sound when people who are rarely heard decide to grab the microphone and start telling everybody how it is. When people vote against their own interests because they don't think it's going to matter either way. People who are then called 'arseholes' and 'scum' by middle class liberals for expressing genuine shock that their vote actually did bring about change – for the first time in their lives. Luckily, the 'liberal intelligentsia' and the 'metropolitan elite' possess enough influence, cultural capital and personal agency to construct their own vast parallel reality in the event that coarse, under class concerns do start bleeding into the conversation. A parallel reality where 'twibbons', safety-pins, free-hugs, *Huffington Post* think-pieces, Tumblr blogs and gender-neutral gingerbread products are all that's needed to resolve a crisis. When the full wrath of working class anger is brought to bear on the domain of politics, sending ripples through our culture, it's treated like a national disaster. Following these political earthquakes, a deluge of condescending, patronising and emotionally hysterical social media posts, blogs and online campaigns are launched, ruminating about the extinction level event – which is what is declared whenever this specialist class, on the left or right, get a vague sense that they are no longer calling the shots. That they have been defied. That culture is no longer being curated with them in mind. For these people, not getting their way feels like abuse.

The morning of Brexit, multiple crises were announced simultaneously by middle class liberals, progressives and radicals, who were suddenly confronted with the vulgar and divided country the rest of us had been living in for decades. A country filled with violence and racism. A country where people had become so alienated by the mainstream conversation that they were beginning to create their own parallel cultures and even their own 'alternative facts'. It was infuriating to witness one hyperventilating *Guardian* subscriber after the other, lamenting how a once-great nation had gone to the dogs.

Of course, by 'dogs' they meant the working class.

In the week following Brexit, I was operating in several communities across the city, all with high migrant populations. However, contrary to the pronouncements of many people on social media, who took the liberty of announcing Armageddon on everybody's behalf, immigrants and the poor were very calm. Life continued as normal. Local people organised cultural diversity events in solidarity with migrants and refugees. Gazebos were erected in parks to distribute micro-grants to local groups. Young people attended music lessons in youth clubs held in churches – not a journalist in site.

In these communities, it was just another week. Here, violence is present every day – it doesn't 'spike'. Here, racism is a horrible fact of life – it isn't 'unleashed'. Of course, many foreign nationals were very anxious about what this referendum result would mean for their citizenship in the UK. Many people of colour received horrendous racial abuse from morons who took Brexit as a green light to engage in bullying and hooliganism. It was perfectly appropriate that communities moved quickly to acknowledge those fears and to show unconditional solidarity with those affected. But much of the outrage that was flying around had nothing to do with what immigrants actually thought or felt; it was about people using those issues to conceal their own naked classism.

Thankfully, in the following days and weeks this group of well-meaning millennials managed to compose themselves, exercising tremendous personal restraint by comparing the experience of not getting their way in a vote, to fascism and accusing anyone who thought that was a bit over the top of apologising for Nazis.

22

The Way We Live Now

ONE OF THE main themes in Pollok in the early '90s, during the period of heightened political participation, was the issue of public space; who owns it and who has the power to make decisions about what happens to it? Back then, it was regarded as paranoid to think these public spaces were being deliberately receded to make way for private developers, but nearly 20 years later this paranoia has been vindicated. But as is usually the case, nobody takes the time to acknowledge that the people in these poorer communities were, in fact, correct. Life simply continues as if nothing has happened. Think of the manager or colleague who, after hearing one of your ideas or observations, passes it off as their own at the next staff meeting and is commended by everyone for their foresight. Being underclass is to sit, day after day, and scroll through a news feed full of *Guardian* articles that are confirming things you knew were the case 20 years prior. 'Study finds children living in dysfunction can't learn', 'Experts say sugar is addictive' or, my personal favourite, 'Survey discovers the arts is dominated by middle class people'. If only there was a way of getting the people who shape the narrative, to check in with the people at the bottom of the food chain every now and then. It might interrupt the steady stream of assumptions many affluent assertions are based on and bring the conversation about society into sync with how society is really being experienced. But as well as being mildly irritating or causing people to feel excluded or misrepresented, these assumptions, well meaning as they often are, can also prove pretty costly both financially and culturally.

In the Gorbals one of the key assumptions in the post-war

regeneration phase was that all people needed was a decent place to live. The high-rise building programme and housing schemes were the solution to what was regarded as mainly a housing problem. What planners later realised was that people also required a sense of ownership, a stake and connectedness in their communities, as well as adequate living standards. And we all learned the hard way that highly populated areas, where people are deprived of connection, stake and ownership, can quickly fall into physical and psychological dereliction. But providing this connectedness is easier said than done. In fact, it has become one of the biggest challenges facing areas where significant numbers of people feel socially isolated, despite the proliferation of social media and technology, and have withdrawn from community life. One of the reasons for this is that there are fewer public spaces for them to go to – unless they have money.

In Pollok, the Silverburn (and shopping malls like it) attempts to supply the human need for stake, ownership and connection. But for all the benefits of such a place, much of what is on offer is illusory and fleeting. Consumer communities are exclusive; you need to spend money regularly to be granted access. And as for a feeling of ownership, you might experience an elevated sense of autonomy when you leave the shop with your new trainers, but just try hanging around for too long without buying something else and you'll soon learn who the place really belongs to. These malls should function as an extension of a community – not as its centre.

It's partly because of these consumer villages, and how they have literally set up shop in the centre of our communities, that we tend to associate the word 'centre' with a physical entity such as a building or a designated space. A 'centre' is usually a structure that contains rooms or offices where people gather, work or mingle. If it's not a building, then it's an area for people to occupy at their leisure. However, when you consider the word 'centre', not as a noun but as a verb, it can have a profound impact on your conception of what a community centre can be.

Or, more to the point, what it ought to be.

Rather than merely providing warmth, shelter or access to

space or activities, a community centre can orientate, engage, educate and inspire people, creating a higher vibration of community consciousness and shared purpose that often leads to increased wellbeing, higher quality of life and, ultimately, social cohesion. However, if you walk into any community centre in your town or city then what you are likely to find is a once proud local institution breathing its heart-breaking agonal gasp.

Tonight, at a community centre on the southside of Glasgow, some young people have arrived to play football. The game is quickly abandoned when youth workers realise they can't provide a ball. One of the boys runs home to get his own ball. When he returns, he complains that it's flat. Youth workers can't provide a pump to blow it up. Half the boys who turned up, keen for a game, leave abruptly and begin causing disruption outside the community centre. The remaining group are invited to another room to take part in activities. Activities which include playing old, damaged PlayStation games with broken control pads. If that doesn't float your boat, there's always the table tennis – without a table – where nets are fixed clumsily to wooden desks, before the game is abandoned due to being unplayable. Sometimes kids just hit the ping-pong ball to each other for fun.

Along the corridor, a playgroup has just started for children between the ages of 5 and 12. It's a 'Toy Library', set up for children who live in poverty, where they can access high quality toys and games for free. Kids sign the toy out for a few days and when they bring it back they can take another one. But before the scheme got off the ground, the roof collapsed and the club was closed for months. In youth clubs, young people play pool on wonky tables with cues that have no tips. When the table gives out, it won't be fixed or replaced for months. When it is replaced, it is assembled wrong and can't be used for weeks. Staff bring in their own property, or purchase items like computer games, arts and crafts material and batteries with their own money to provide an acceptable level of service. Children turn up to take part in activities that have been advertised that youth workers either haven't been informed about or have no resources to provide. There is a constant sense that nobody really knows what is going on; that every conversation you have with a manager is inconsequential. The saddest thing of all is that there is a high demand for these services and a skilled, passionate team of youth workers desperate to engage. But the services have fallen so far behind in terms of what youth culture entails in the digital age, that young people have stopped coming because the quality on offer is so inconsistent. Worse still, when public sector workers live in a constant state of job insecurity, they are constrained in terms of what they can say and do to address the problems. The issues are swept under the rug, ignored or simply forgotten, because people know that saying something may be more hassle than its worth.

If that's not your idea of a good time, then the only other place you can go in the community where you won't be expected to spend money, is the library. However, the library has also undergone some pretty fundamental changes. It's being gradually repurposed, by the back door, as replacement for the ailing community centre which is being used more and more for commercial purposes and leased out to other organisations, groups and facilitators. In the sector, this is regarded as a smart idea because it addresses the fact that less people use libraries and also the fact community centres are often not fit for purpose. To justify keeping the library service running, local authorities have had to open them up to third sector organisations looking for cheap space, as well as public services, like mother and toddler groups. Increasingly, the local library is being pitched as a multi-purpose drop-in centre; a hybrid of a community centre and a library. It must be said that such a hybrid is not necessarily a bad idea if that were the original concept. Such a service would be quite revolutionary in a city like Glasgow, for example. But that's not what's happening here. Essentially, the community centre is being imposed on the library to streamline the service in order to justify keeping the library open. This practice undermines the integrity of both the library and the community centre. It undermines the principle that communities should be entitled to these vital amenities independent of one another. In these areas, it's not just public space that is receding, it's the very principle that it should exist at all.

Admittedly, many of us don't use libraries anymore, but for those who do, it's impossible to overstate how indispensable the service is. Particularly in communities characterised by poor education, low opportunity and high levels of stress, the library is an engine room of social mobility where people go to complete college and job applications, get help filling out forms to access benefits and bursaries as well as accessing internet and books to learn new skills or find information. People who enter a library are actively trying to better themselves in some way and often lack the basic resources or skills to reach their goals. When you are in a public library, you are in the presence of people who are attempting to take a massive stride forward in their often chaotic and stressful lives. Aside from this more obvious function, the library performs a much simpler one – one which any librarian worth their salt will guard jealously. As well as not costing any money, the library is one of the few places in a deprived community that is quiet enough to hear yourself think.

To get a sense of how difficult it is to concentrate when there are things going on around you, pick up your smart phone and start thumbing through a selection of ring tones, while continuing to read this page – I'll wait. Now imagine you are already pretty stressed, perhaps because you have no money, or because debt collectors and council tax are breathing down your neck. Now throw in the fact you are maybe not the best reader. Maybe you are a single mum, with a learning difficulty like dyslexia, or you might be battling with a drink problem. Maybe you're looking to get back into education and have a limited amount of time for activities that require concentration? Maybe you are a young man, recently released from prison, perhaps on a tag, who has been given an apprenticeship in a barbers or local deli but have no experience? Throw a little ADHD in the mix and an underlying psychological issue, which is exacerbated by stress, and suddenly the simple act of entering a library becomes an immense act of personal courage.

Walking into a library is often the first step a person takes out of social exclusion, unemployment and poverty. When you don't live this kind of precarious life every day then it's easy to forget that many other people do – and it's bloody hellish. For many of the people who depend on libraries, there are already enough barriers in place – economic, cultural and social – to dissuade them from even attempting to try something as challenging as filling out an application form, disputing a sanction from the Job Centre or learning to read.

Then we have the senior citizen, largely forgotten in the beard-stroking dither of progressive politics. Perhaps a widow who lives alone, or a disabled man who uses a wheelchair and can only access a certain number of buildings in the area. The library is one of the only places they'll be allowed to stop for more than five minutes without being expected to spend money. And let's not forget, there's a reason people in areas like this need to get out of their homes every now and then: paper-thin walls that mean you can hear your neighbours flushing toilets, boiling kettles, having sex, arguing, doing DIY, cutting their grass, revving their cars – at every hour of the day. This is not to mention the less-than-serene sounds of a stressful community, and all the challenging, often frightening, behaviour it fuels; couples engaged in aggressive disputes, drunken young people shouting in the streets, strangers coming and going all day and night. Not to mention the regular sound of police cars, ambulances and fire engines.

The library is one of many dwindling resources, like the community centre, that act as safety valves. A library provides a safe and supportive environment where vulnerable people can educate themselves or mentally regroup. But increasingly, they will arrive at the library to find children running around, or people taking part in discussions or courses, or Mother/Toddler groups. These activities are equally essential – but they should be going on in a community centre. Libraries have become busy, often quite noisy places, which seriously defeats their intended purpose. Councils are under increasing pressure to maintain a high level of service with fewer resources at their disposal and the axe is falling on the services with the least capacity for resilience. How odd that in the social pressure cooker of a deprived community, characterised by chronic stress and low educational attainment, something as simple and vital as a quiet place to be with your thoughts has become such an unreasonable expectation.

There was a time when the authorities could get away with this stuff. Times are a-changing – and not for the better. In these communities, stress levels are so high and people feel so aggrieved about having their concerns dismissed and ignored, that the usual methods of pacifying their anger are failing. Now people are not only angry, but also less likely to be interested in lectures about how to express that anger.

Stressful social conditions have a psychological impact on everyone who is subject to them. Over time, they change the way people behave. This, in turn, changes the shape and direction of a community. Anger and resentment, fertilised by the deeper psychological challenges associated with poverty – anxiety, depression, poor lifestyle and low self-esteem, social insecurity – place a significant emotional strain on everyone. This strain can limit human capacity for empathy, tolerance and compassion and makes many people angry, agitated, resentful and frightened. Now, with the rise in xenophobia and racism, and the rhetoric that stokes this prejudice, it is not hard to see where many who spend every day of their lives in these conditions have wrongly decided to turn their anger. This is what happens in a community with no centre.

23

Housekeeping

POVERTY NOT ONLY expresses itself in the behaviour and lifestyles of the poor, but also in their social attitudes. Apathy is a big one. Scepticism of authority and public institutions is another. People are raised in homes where nobody believes they can effect change and they grow up internalising those beliefs. The apathy of the poor, in terms of politics, is so apparent that it's factored into political calculations: leaders pitch policy to those who are more likely to participate. This, in turn, creates a cycle where the interests of those who do not participate are not considered, which leads to more apathy. But every now and then, when things are at breaking point, social deprivation vomits up an antidote to apathy.

It's one of the paradoxes of poverty: the harder things get, the more resilient some people become. Cultures of resistance are forged on the anvil of social deprivation and for every person who withers in poverty's wake, another grows more resolute and determined. Social deprivation can tear communities apart, but it can also renew them because it forces people to cooperate, innovate and evolve to find the solutions to their common problems.

The rise of foodbanks across the UK perhaps best encapsulates this paradox. On one hand, it's morally outrageous that in a country of such undoubted prosperity people should have to access foodbanks to feed their children or face going without themselves. But those very foodbanks, rather than merely conduits of charity, have become fiefdoms within deprived communities, around which people become engaged and organised. It's an uncomfortable truth of poverty and of life generally: struggle forces us to evolve. After nearly a decade of austerity, something is stirring again in the schemes, estates and housing projects of the west. What form it will take is not yet clear, but there is a battle going on for the soul of working class communities. People are beginning to organise and just like Pollok in the '90s, the generals are not mainstream politicians, but local people themselves, coming together in spite of them. Castlemilk is a district on Glasgow's south side that was developed as a 'housing scheme' in the 1950s. But as we know, the well-intended promise of the housing scheme was never fulfilled. For many it quickly turned into a living nightmare and by the '80s had become synonymous with crime, drugs and violence. The anger and scepticism that built in communities like Castlemilk over successive decades, not only due to poor social conditions but also because of the lack of opportunity to escape them, became a volatile cultural energy, oscillating between anger and apathy, that many movements have since tried to politicise in the hope of harnessing it for electoral purposes. The sudden interest in the daily plight of the 'working class', 'lower class' and 'the poor' always seems to peak in the run-up to an election (or a referendum). This interest quickly peters out. Once the politicians get power, they retreat into their privileged political spheres. This pattern has been duly noted by locals, who are often privately regarded by politicians as lacking the necessary sophistication to do politics right.

'I'm not a politician,' says Cathy Milligan, a 53-year-old community activist who grew up in Castlemilk. Cathy recently ran as an independent in the local elections. She, along with a core group of community activists, founded Castlemilk Against Austerity (CAA) in 2014. The fact that Cathy is not a politician is currently her biggest asset, though how long that will remain the case is anybody's guess. Political figures are not highly regarded in communities like this. Cathy is wise to disassociate herself from the word 'politician', rather as Joe from The Barn rejected the term 'manager' – they both know these words arouse suspicion and scepticism. For now, Cathy Milligan is a woman of the people. She is not only visible in the area but also fluent in the local language and customs, which are often regarded as coarse, vulgar, offensive or abusive by many of the politicos and activists who parachute in looking for scraps of political capital. Cathy is intuitive, not only to the day-to-day concerns of locals, but to how people express those concerns and how the disparate challenges in the community can coalesce in outbursts of apathy, anger and, increasingly, racism and xenophobia.

'The root of racism is austerity,' says Cathy, unambiguously. 'People on benefits turn against others on benefits. If you're backed into a corner it brings out the worst in you. As human beings, we know how to make things better for each other but the economics of austerity stops all that. We're under the cosh and we're fighting for our lives.'

'Fighting for their lives' is not an exaggeration. For many people in Castlemilk, poverty will be the indirect cause of death. What makes Cathy so endearing is that her intelligence is not marshalled in service of an agenda to harness local anger for her own ends. Instead, Cathy represents a nurturing, caring force. She encourages people to rediscover their self-belief and take responsibility for the upkeep of their own community. Cathy recognises that capacity in the community, emotionally and socially, is very low and that there will be no meaningful change until people become more active, engaged and resilient. This resilience is not only about belief in political participation, but also about resisting the temptation to ascribe blame for poverty on the popular scapegoats of immigrants and drug addicts. Cathy is resigned to the reality that the age of austerity may continue for many years but is adamant that people stand up and be counted rather than see themselves as helpless victims: 'We're not saying we have all the answers. But we're smart enough to figure it out. We believe in each other and we believe in the community.'

In one month alone, CAA ran a variety of campaigns and events that took a holistic view of community needs and aspirations. In Castlemilk, they understand that it takes more than chants of 'Tory scum' to bring about the sort of shift in thinking required to reorganise a community. Whether it be the food solidarity programmes (they don't call them foodbanks here) aimed at reducing the social stigma associated with food poverty, leaflets designed to push back against racism and xenophobia, or seminars about the impact of bullying, CAA are charging on with a lack of concern for the agendas of political parties or activists jockeying for banner positions at anti-Trump rallies. Obviously everyone is welcome, but people have been warned about who is really running things around here.

In fact, talk of Trump and Brexit is viewed here as a distraction. At a recent screening of Ken Loach's *I, Daniel Blake*, the award winning drama about the UK sanctions regime, Glasgow poet and activist Robert Fullertone – who writes the sort of poetry you won't find in a school curriculum – clipped me around the proverbial ear for mentioning Donald Trump during a panel discussion. 'Are you out there, Trump?' he joked, his gesture towards the door perhaps alluding to the perma-tanned egotist's role as a bogeyman for radical socialists and left-wing groups. Such groups, in recent years, have struggled to find their voice as nationalist folds have emerged across the fabric of society. But the rallies and stunts they often engage in to boost morale and visibility have created cynicism and irritation among the very working class people they are hoping to mobilise. The left is no longer assumed to be comprised exclusively of good guys. Fullertone, as eloquent a public speaker as you are likely to hear, believes the obsession with Trump and Brexit has become just another side-show that detracts from the struggle taking place in his community.

While many on the cultural left – who've come to dominate the liberal institutions of the arts, the media, the public and third sector as well as our universities – appear capable only of blaming right-wing conservatives for everything, increasing numbers in communities like Castlemilk are just as hacked off with the left as they are with everyone else. But, as well as this outward anger at the system, at those whom they feel ignored or abandoned by, there is a growing desire for self-scrutiny here too.

This urge to challenge themselves, as well as everyone else, is not only admirable but extremely practical. They understand that externalising blame for their circumstances while remaining inactive is simply just another way of handing their agency to the opportunists, sowing yet more seeds of apathy down the line. Castlemilk Against Austerity, while adamant that austerity politics is making life harder, doesn't spin a 'poor us' narrative. Instead, as well as organising to resist the system, they challenge the community to examine its own shortcomings and false beliefs. They recognise the link between belief and action that creates the conditions for apathy, anger and prejudice. Whether it be blaming immigrants for social problems or paying lip-service to wanting change while sitting on your hands and doing nothing, CAA are on the front line, calling out bull***t wherever it is found.

Addressing a packed hall in Kinning Park, Fullertone didn't mince his words: 'The problem with our politics right now is none of us are doing it. It's no good enough to go up the road after this event, thrilled at what's been said. You've got to go and do it. My back is killing me tonight, I've lost my inhaler and I'm short of breath, but that never stops me walking slow – to where the battle is.'

The battle is on his doorstep, on his street and up his close. In these communities, you'll find the real foot soldiers in the fight against the far-right ideas breaking in as the cracks begin to show in these historically stressed communities. Here, if you want to challenge a racist it's a little trickier than writing a blog or composing a condemnatory tweet – although all forms of resistance have their place. Here you can really put yourself in harm's way, not only by challenging racists but by being consistently visible doing it. At grassroots level, it's not as simple as instigating a social media witch-hunt against people who behave offensively. In Castlemilk, and areas like it, simply condemning people is not an option. Here, the war of ideas is messy and coarse and sometimes even shocking. People work out their differences in a way the poetry of the school curriculum hasn't quite managed to capture. Robert Fullertone commands the room, not only as an orator, but as an elder, a sage and a leader. But in political circles, or in activist communities with a different entry level into the conversation, a guy like Robert may be regarded as a bit vulgar, rough around the edges or – my personal favourite – too angry.

But he speaks the sort of powerful, heartfelt rhetoric that gets you in the gut. He has a way with words that politicos across the spectrum have tried – and failed – to mimic. CAA, who launched a crowdfund to raise a modest £1,000 to fight the local election, will likely be shouted down or sneered at by various sections of the public. The xenophobes will think Cathy an apologist for the crimes of immigrants, regarded by many as undeserving of help or compassion while so many of the 'indigenous' population struggles. Others will see this attempt to enter the political arena as a distraction from a worthier pursuit, either party political or nationalist. And the rest will conclude it's a waste of time and energy because things never change.

I suspect that when faced with the sheer power of the message Cathy and Robert are carrying, which is as much about challenging themselves and the community as it is about rallying against the system, then those who would sneer will come to bow their heads for fear of drawing their gaze. Down here, life is very real and people can cut you down with a shooting glance. As services are cut and apathy sets in, while the endless debate rages on in political circles, it's the people like Cathy and Robert, who refuse to lie down and play victims or to allow their fellows to scapegoat the vulnerable, that show people there is another way to live.

They become the new centre of the community. Sadly, however, not every community has a Cathy or a Robert to fill the void.

24

Waiting for the Barbarians

WHEN YOU TAKE a strong dislike to someone, everything they say or do becomes irritating and suspect. Once you have decided, either due to something you've read, something you've been told or a direct interaction you've had, that you can no longer abide a certain someone, you begin subconsciously building your case against them. It might not even be a person but a place, an institution, an idea or a belief. No matter what form the source of your annoyance takes, you will hold it in a progressively lower regard and find common cause with others who've arrived at a similar conclusion. Those who appear to show sympathy, solidarity or support for the subject of your contempt will be exiled from your consideration and recategorised as mere extensions of the thing you've grown to hate. This is the emotional reality in which much of our current political debate is rooted. Given the sheer scale of bad faith exhibited, in debates on any number of issues, across the political spectrum, it's a bit rich to pretend it's only racists and xenophobes who are unfairly dehumanising sections of the population. I grew up calling Conservatives 'scum' and genuinely believing it, oblivious to the broad spectrum of Conservative opinion that exists. Others in my community claim 'all cops are bastards' – even the ones who run towards knife-wielding terrorists to protect the public. From a very young age, we are all inculcated into the mores of a tribe and adopt those values often without thought, later mistaking them for our own.

The biggest feature of the tribalism that has come to characterise our culture is the belief in the legitimacy of our own resentments. We see ourselves as complex thinkers, arriving at conclusions through careful reasoning, believing those with whom we disagree to be motivated by stupidity and prejudice. Oddly, we miss the fact our mental process is almost identical to theirs, regardless of the nobility of the cause we believe ourselves to be advancing. Belief in the virtue of our own hypocrisy is one of the few things we have in common in this increasingly divided society.

Recently, I saw a striking example of where this kind of thinking leads when I attended an additional needs school in Scotland. I was invited there to work with two teenagers who were presenting a challenge to youth workers. The boys had been refusing to take part in any tasks and persisted in scrolling through their phones during lessons.

This school, tucked away in one of Glasgow's many schemes, is for young people whose 'additional needs' can be physical, such as using a wheelchair, learning difficulties like dyslexia, or stress related conditions like ADHD. Today, my job is to 'engage' two young boys who are already well on their way to complete social exclusion.

The energy in the room is flat. Everyone has reverted to type: the boys are confrontational, the staff are resorting to the language of disciplinarians. I'm here to shake things up a bit, but I am in a foul mood.

A house move and working multiple jobs while trying to finish a book is extremely stressful. I have barely slept, my stomach turns like a washing machine full of grievances; some justified, some unfair, the rest baseless. For two weeks, I have been privately fantasising about using drugs. Today the reality that I am an addict seems so distant. Almost like a dream. Memories I would normally cringe at in sobriety, like drinking on a bus or raiding a bin for a cigarette butt, now warm my heart in a sudden rush of nostalgia. It's the same process of delusion that landed me in McDonald's earlier today, or on a porn site last night, or with a pocket full of chocolate this morning. A sense of emotional discomfort or stress creates an urge I find hard to disobey. I am considering the very real possibility of a relapse.

I am stressed out, tired, angry and absolutely fed up, so I know exactly what these boys are going through. My ability to bring all of myself to work, and not just a professional persona, is why engaging with difficult people like this is something I know I am really good at. To try and build a rapport, I firstly ask them to draw a mind map – a spider diagram for gathering ideas. Given I don't know a lot about them I suggest a topic they are likely to have some foreknowledge of: Glasgow, the city in which they live.

'It's a shite-hole,' says one, giving the standard response from children of this age and from this kind of area, who regard their own communities as dysfunctional, dirty and defective.

'Fulla junkies,' says the other.

'What else annoys you about Glasgow?' I ask.

'Immigrants,' says one, to which the other nods in agreement.

'What is it about immigrants that annoys you?' I ask.

'They come here and take jobs and houses when we have enough homeless people on our streets.'

'They rape people.'

'They shouldn't be allowed to speak in their own language.'

'If they are running away from a war then maybe they should stay in their own countries and fight?'

'If they hate Britain then why come here?'

Within two minutes, these normally mute, unresponsive, passive-aggressive boys suddenly spring to life and reveal to me an issue they are not only passionate about but clearly believe themselves to be knowledgeable on. It's just a shame they are racist.

Racist attitudes like these, often learned at home, are carried into adulthood before being passed on to the next generation. Which is why many are anxious about conceding ground to people with 'legitimate' concerns about immigration.

25

The Naked Ape

NOT EVERYONE WITH concerns about immigration should be dismissed as a racist, but taking this on board could be seen as opening the door to the worst kind of xenophobia. It is vital not to oversimplify expressions of racism or fail to drill down into its real causes and so what I will attempt to outline here is the beginning of a strategy to confront anti-immigration sentiment at its roots. This approach recognises that the racist component in any anti-immigration sentiment must be challenged and condemned. Nevertheless, confronting such a complicated social problem means facing up to what some will consider unpalatable truths and addressing the psychosocial drivers that can underpin racist views.

It is counterproductive to hold the view that anyone with concerns about immigration must be misinformed, racist or stupid. For instance, I find the word 'junkie' quite offensive, but if I decided I wasn't going to listen to the opinion of anyone who used that word, I'd only be creating more problems for myself – especially if my goal is to create better dialogue around the issue. Sometimes, much as it pains us, we must grudgingly adjust ourselves to reality before seeking to reorder it. Superimposing our own values on other people, in the hope of corralling them to our way of thinking, is not only naive, it is futile.

This is especially the case when dealing with massive dispar-ities in experience, because the person we think of as racist is as firmly rooted in the reality of their own moral world as someone of an opposing view. Now let me be clear, this is not an attempt to claim there is an automatic moral equivalence between any two opposing viewpoints. It's simply to acknowledge that, because of their background and upbringing, people tend to commit to their beliefs irrespective of the veracity of the beliefs themselevs. Therefore, the fear of being publicly shamed or condemned outwith that community is unlikely to convince anyone to change their position. On top of which, it is likely that condemnation will arouse suspicion and scepticism – emotions that close the possibility of dialogue. Moral outrage and condemnation, however justified and cathartic, is likely to be a waste of energy if the objective is to encourage a change of mind. To me, this is the reality of the challenge in respect of immigration as a political issue.

The dilemma of where debate breaks down is analysed in forensic detail by American scholar and psychologist Jonathan Haidt in his book *The Righteous Mind: Why Good People are Divided by Politics and Religion*. His examination of the interplay of biology, neuroscience, evolution and psychology suggests that finding common ground between warring political factions requires mindfulness of the extent to which instinct drives politics. He argues that when we find debate intractable, this can be because we are too quick to dismiss – or monster – other points of view. Responses of disgust and revulsion and the social pressure we experience to conform to a political dogma make us less likely to grant opposing views full consideration. While this may ingratiate us with our own political tribe and sharpen our sense of who we are, these factors potentiate dialogue breakdown and even more serious conflict. If we are to bridge those gulfs of understanding and overcome apparently intransigent political and cultural divisions, Haidt sees it as vital to appreciate moral diversity and open channels of dialogue. He writes:

> If you really want to change someone's mind on a moral or political matter, you'll need to see things from that person's angle as well as your own. And if you do truly see it the other person's way – deeply and intuitively – you might even find your own mind opening in response... empathy is an antidote to righteousness, although it's very difficult to empathise across a moral divide.

And so, if we genuinely want to confront and reverse racism and xenophobia, we must expand the armoury of tools at our disposal. The campaign of shaming has failed. Our proclamations about tolerance, diversity and inclusion will require an enhanced component of emotional literacy. There is a new emotional reality that we must integrate into our understanding if we are to truly confront this issue, as opposed to merely containing it. The reality is that the conditions of poverty in which much of this (though certainly not all) anti-immigration sentiment is found are so severe they affect the way people think, feel and behave. Granted, resistance, condemnation and censorship may culturally suppress the worst of it, creating the impression it has dissipated, but the issue will re-emerge in a more virulent form further down the line

Obviously, not everyone will be prepared to act from this point of view, but those of us who are willing to try, must – even at the risk of criticism and expulsion from our own tribe. Everyone must be free to hold to their strict ethical lines but it is also crucial that those who wish are free to explore the grey areas between seemingly black and white moral issues.

It's also important to resist making value judgements based solely on the language people use when expressing an opinion; when someone expresses what appears to be a racist opinion, there are several factors to be considered before that person can truly be dismissed as a racist. When someone prefaces their opinion with 'I'm not racist, but', they might be telling the truth. Then there's the social and cultural context and personal circumstances to consider. Take the two boys I mentioned in the previous chapter. Would condemnation from me have served any purpose, other than removing the potential for dialogue later? In practical terms, what would calling those young boys racist really have achieved, especially if they do not recognise my moral authority, and being regarded as racist by me is not a problem for them?

Endeavouring to make distinctions between different sorts of anti-immigration sentiment is not a matter of choice, it is a matter of practical urgency – and has nothing to do with apologising for regressive social attitudes or condoning racist views. On the contrary, it's about engaging in a serious and robust way. Patience, tolerance and cultural sophistication are needed as much as condemnation and moral outrage. This approach means disengaging temporarily from our own sense of what is right and wrong and opening ourselves to the moral logic of people with whom we disagree.

In my experience, many people arrive at conclusions that could be characterised as racist, or express views in a racist manner, either because of their upbringing or because the only people prepared to listen to them happen to be bigots. But this does not mean they can't be persuaded otherwise, in the right circumstances. Writing someone off as racist implies they are unsalvageable and futureless; that they are beyond hope. Outright condemnation risks reinforcing the feelings of exclusion that push people into the arms of the far right. In the instance of those young boys in the additional needs school, condemning them as racist would have been about as useful as reading a newspaper to a piece of fruit. I believe that whatever the context, a nuanced approach to anti-immigration is required and that every person requires a different approach before they are tossed into the bucket of deplorables.

Sometimes people are drawn to right-wing figures like Donald Trump and Nigel Farage because they feel they are finally being listened to; they feel they are striking back at the people they feel abandoned and excluded by. Sometimes that urge to retaliate takes precedence over all other concerns. Yet in the western world, the fact that immigration is a mainstream issue has had little impact in some quarters. Many on the left believe that conceding even an inch is to open the door to fascism. Others are engaged in a campaign of denial and obfuscation where the facts about immigration are concerned. People who are unwilling to concede or discuss some of the uncomfortable truths about immigration fall into two camps: those who know there are problems but who believe it's dangerous to discuss them in terms set by the far right, and those who genuinely don't think there's an issue and that anyone who does is racist.

Let me reiterate: the threat posed by right-wing populism is very real. But to claim there are no legitimate concerns about immigration is useless and fails to account for the extent to which politics are rooted in the emotional reality of people's lives.

Unsurprisingly, the people in society who are pro-immigration are usually those who feel connected, involved or have been cut into the action in some way and are thus invested in the process. It's in their interests, personally, professionally and culturally, to talk up the merits of immigration and dissuade anti-immigration sentiment. They belong to networks and social circles that grant insight into how decisions are made and may even be able to affect the outcome of these decisions in some way. Pro-immigration third sector groups, charities, activists and politicians are quick to talk up the 'net gains' of immigration, unlike those who are frozen out of these networks. Net gains are rarely felt this far down the economic pecking order, so it's a bit of a red herring as far as persuasive arguments go.

As I outlined earlier, being locked out of the decision-making process lies at the heart of a lot of community friction. In terms of immigration, the far right emerges in various forms to capitalise on the vacuum left by those who refuse to engage with this issue.

It's not rocket science: listen, and those who feel ignored will re-engage passionately. People used to being dismissed will form bonds of trust with the individuals, movements, organisations and political parties that include them. This creates the social electricity that can be harnessed for positive political momentum. If we can change our posture towards some of the anti-immigration sentiment and engage it, many will begin to believe there is value in dialogue and turn away from the far right, which preys on anger and exclusion as political propulsion.

Racism exists at every level of society. It would be wrong to argue otherwise or imply that poverty absolves people of taking responsibility for their socially regressive attitudes or hate crimes. Anxieties about legitimising racism are completely justified. Bigots, emboldened by the social divisions so evident in our society, will exploit every opportunity to empower themselves. But the danger of dismissing concerns about immigration offhand, or failing to appreciate the varying degrees of concern being expressed and its broader context, is that people are excluded from the conversation about their own lives.

I know I'm probably being a bit naive and overly optimistic, but I find it really hard to write-off people living in deprived areas as unsalvageable or futureless for pointing out some of the obvious problems in their community. Yes, it's wrong that people should pin blame on immigrants themselves, but it's not wrong to admit that immigration policy can have immensely challenging impacts in socially deprived communities. Acknowledging this might disarm much of the criticism currently being levelled at the left, which is regarded as impossibly idealistic on this issue.

We need to look at the impact spikes in the migrant population have on deprived communities where psychosocial stress is already endemic. We cannot decide to acknowledge or ignore social concerns or problems purely on the basis of whether we feel personally offended or threatened. Not every degree of concern about immigration is the same and anybody with a genuine interest in social justice must be prepared to hear what people have to say before dismissing them as racist. If we can accept that criminality or chronic illness often has its roots in poverty then we must also be prepared to accept that other socially regressive attitudes may too. The reason it's so important to make these distinctions is in order to distinguish those we can persuade or accommodate from those we really need to fight. It's not about giving racists a free pass; it's about properly rooting them out and leaving them with nowhere to hide.

Some of the world's most vulnerable people, fleeing poverty and violence, find themselves in our most impoverished and violent communities on arrival in the UK. In the whirlwind of hyperbole, scapegoating and recrimination, there is a sensible conversation to be had about both the causes and effects of immigration in our most challenged communities and how we can make it work better. Not least for migrants themselves.

The Sound and the Fury

AS THE POLITICAL spectrum continues to fracture and alliances are drawn along new lines, large sections of the poorer communities the traditional left believes itself best placed to represent are abandoning it; and this has created an opening for far less inhibited right wing figures, speaking in the abandoned language of class struggle, to ruthlessly exploit.

One big area of contention for the left has been the domain of 'identity politics'.

This family of ideas has a few labels, imported from the States. One is 'intersectionality', which describes how discrimination, based on gender, race and sexual orientation, as well as factors like religion or disabilities, affects individuals and groups. Intersectionality is one of many theories that come under the umbrella of 'social justice'. Social justice ought to be an evolution and diversification of class politics, its scope extending beyond lines of social class and into race, gender and so on. But as intersectionality has become more prominent, class analysis has been discarded. Rather than a class politics which accounts for a broader range of people, social justice in the mould of identity politics gentrifies traditional class-based analysis.

In December 2016 on *Bella Caledonia*, activist Henry Bell argued in favour of intersectionality. His short polemic, 'In Defence of Identity Politics', maintains that privileging class struggle over others conceals, and thus perpetuates, the sub-cultures of oppression which undermine equality, and that, while imperfect, identity politics offers us the best possible opportunity to develop an inclusive dialogue. Bell writes:

The left's insistence for more than a century that class struggle was more important than any other oppression and that its destruction would lead to the destruction of these other systems of control alienated a majority of people. It was also a lie. It served to preserve structures of racism and patriarchy within our own movement. If we don't acknowledge the privileges and oppressions that we enact, then we will not be able to destroy them.

The problem is that Bell presents critics of intersectionality with a false choice: accept it, or return to the toxic machismo of 20th century class politics. Yes, oppression exists; and it's also true that class politics, like every area of life in the West, has been traditionally dominated by white men. But identity politics has become synonymous with a style of activism that many people across the political spectrum find illiberal, censorious and counter-productive. And I am one of them.

Take one of the main ingredients of identity politics: 'call-out culture'. A call-out is the practice of publicly reprimanding someone, usually online. Call-outs are sometimes accompanied by 'no-platforming', which is to pressure an organisation or institution to ban certain individuals from public speaking. Contentious in themselves, these methods tend to obscure the causes they are supposed to be supporting. These issues are highlighted by Toronto based writer Asam Ahmed in 'A Note on Call-out Culture', published in March 2015 in *Briarpatch* magazine. Ahmed writes:

> It isn't an exaggeration to say that there is a mild totalitarian undercurrent not just in call-out culture but also in how progressive communities police and define the bounds of who's in and who's out. More often than not, this boundary is constructed through the use of appropriate language and terminology – a language and terminology that are forever shifting and almost impossible to keep up with. In such a context, it is impossible not to fail at least some of the time.

And what happens when someone has mastered proficiency in languages of accountability and then learned to justify all of their actions by falling back on that language? How do we hold people to account who are experts at using anti-oppressive language to justify oppressive behaviour? We don't have a word to describe this kind of perverse exercise of power, despite the fact it occurs on an almost daily basis in progressive circles.

Activist communities, particularly those that develop on university campuses, frequently conflate criticism of identity politics with denial that oppression and inequality exists. The central feature of the identity politics approach to issues of social justice is that it relies primarily on victim and minority group narratives as a form of cultural propulsion; a Trojan horse to advance the political agenda. Any challenge to this form of activistm runs the risk of being reframed as an attack on the minority groups or abuse victims the campaign claims to represent. Debate becomes intractable, not by accident, but by design.

In 'Why This Radical Leftist is Disillusioned by Leftist Culture', activist Bailey Lemon touches on this issue from the perspective of a woman as well as a leftist. The piece was widely read and shared online by others on the left, who felt it echoed their experience. Lemon writes:

> I'm tired of the cliques, the hierarchies, the policing of others, and the power imbalances that exist between people who claim to be friends and comrades. I am exhausted and saddened by the fact that any type of disagreement or difference of opinion in an activist circle will lead to a fight, which sometimes includes abandonment of certain people, deeming them 'unsafe' as well as public shaming and slander. It is disgusting that we claim to be building a new world, a new society, a better way of dealing with social problems – but if a person makes a mistake, says and/or does something wrong, they are not even given a chance to

explain their side of what happened because the process of conflict resolution is in itself driven by ideology rather than a willingness to understand facts. Actually, in today's activist circles one is lucky to be given any sort of due process at all, while everyone is put under social pressure to believe everything they are told regardless of what actually occurred in a given situation. This is not freedom. This is not social justice. There is nothing 'progressive' or 'radical' about it.

Those who believe identity politics is the only way to guarantee inclusive discussion have little to say about its more pernicious tendencies. Rather, its supporters tend to ascribe criticism to disgruntled, 'butt-hurt', misogynistic white men who just can't handle having their privilege checked. In doing so, they speak over the countless women, people of colour, queer, gay and trans people the intersectionality is purportedly designed to empower. Every analysis starts with a privilege check, pre-emptively invalidating the opinions of people who disagree. Pathological oversimplification is not only encouraged but mandatory; responsibility for society's ills is laid at the door of 'straight white males', regardless of social class, who are regarded as the personification of power and privilege.

If intersectionality was applied across the board, we'd gain a fuller picture of the dynamics at play in our multicultural societies – including the intersecting discrimination, prejudice and abuse which takes place between minority groups themselves. Considered taboo or offensive to acknowledge are racism within the LGBT community, homophobia among African Americans, debate about transgenderism in feminist communities, subjugation of women in Muslim communities, domestic violence in lesbian relationships and the neglect or abuse children by their mothers. As well as white male privilege, intersectionality should allow us to better understand the phenomenon of affluent students on the campuses of elite western universities attempting to control how the rest of us think and discuss our own experiences, claiming to speak on our behalf while freezing us out of the conversation.

Instead, when contradictions or anomalies are pointed out, a slew of dismissive or slanderous terms are deployed by activists to dismiss criticisms and curdle any attempt at debate.

Activists will claim that words themselves are a form of violence, while also affording themselves the privilege of engaging in whatever activity they deem necessary in the pursuit of their objectives. Acts of intimidation, harassment and physical violence are seen as valiantly 'punching up'. Every interaction is viewed through an intersectional lens and is, therefore, regarded as a power dynamic. In the grip of heightened emotional states due to social media storms, these activists often become disassociated from the human consequences of their actions. They won't think twice about attempting to ruin a person's reputation or disrupt their employment based on second-hand information or social media gossip. Ultimately, while holding everyone else to account, this culture is itself accountable to no one.

The painful experiences of victims are channelled vicariously by these activists and are used as political battering rams. Meanwhile, to question anything is equated with placing vulnerable people in danger and potentially retraumatising them. This is what gives intersectionality its muscularity, but this style of discourse alienates, silences and disempowers as many people as its galvanises. As a way of perceiving the complexity of our differing experiences as individuals and groups it is undoubtedly very useful. As a practical tool for engaging a broad range of voices in open discussion it is a spectacular failure. The very members of the vulnerable and marginalised communities intersectionality is designed to empower may feel baffled by the jargon, afraid to speak up or ask questions, anxious that they might misspeak and be condemned or exiled. If they do pipe up and say something critical, their opinions are likely to be dismissed as no more than internalised cultural myths perpetuated by their oppressors.

They claim that the oppression and marginalisation of minorities persists because privileged groups remain ignorant as to how their language and behaviour reinforces social exclusion, yet these same activists appear unaware as to how their culturally gated discourse intersects with the lower classes. For many, the term 'working class' has become a synonym for 'white male', making it easier to dismiss the topic of class out of hand – even more so with the recent rise of the Alt-right. White men from lower class backgrounds, many of whom have suffered social exclusion and abuse, become the whipping boys of privileged students. Moreover, activists claim the moral high ground because they purport to place people's lived experience at the heart of everything they do. But this only extends to the approved in-group. If you find yourself on the outside, with an opinion they disagree with, your feelings become inconsequential, something to mock, and your experience as a victim of abuse, trauma or oppression, an afterthought. Identity politics, in this virulent, weaponised and uncommunicative form, selectively elevates the experiences that validate and perpetuate it while minimising – or monstering – the ones that don't.

We hear from advocates of intersectionality that 'capitalism produces oppression and privilege' and that identity politics is the best and most radical mechanism to resist this. Conversely, this strain of agitation for social justice has the full weight of corporate America behind it. Identity politics could not have permeated our culture so proficiently had elites believed it was a threat to their interests. In fact, with global brands like Comedy Central's *The Daily Show*, as well as our own BBC now regularly speaking in the campus-driven language of intersectionality, identity politics has been granted a cultural queue-skip by the very groups it is allegedly designed to challenge.

It's certainly no bad thing that multinational companies like Pepsi, General Electric, Pfizer, Microsoft and Apple are using their clout to advance social justice. But it begs the question: what's in it for them? Intersectionality in its current form, rather than an irritant to privilege, atomises society into competing political factions and undermines what really frightens powerful people: a well organised, educated and unified working class.

Like everything else, identity politics selects for those who are most socially mobile, those who are most able and willing to participate. Even when public life and discourse appears to be more inclusive and diverse because of the extent to which women and minority groups are represented, it tends to be middle class women, middle class members of the LGBT community and middle class people of colour who ascend. Political parties often talk up their progressive credentials by drawing attention to the ethnic minorities in their ranks, but they are less inclined to acknowledge which of those went to private school. Class issues are concealed beneath a progressive veneer as identity politics becomes another vehicle for the socially mobile to dominate every aspect of public life. That said, intersectionality is here to stay and, despite its obvious problems, has much to offer, not least to those who find political participation challenging due to the barriers they face. The ideas and theories promoted – privilege, safe spaces, trigger warnings and gaslighting – despite much of the hyperbole surrounding them, are often useful in helping victims of abuse or oppression develop a language and the self-confidence to articulate their personal experiences. Intersectionality can help people take their first important political steps. But it should never be seen as the answer to every question. Intersectionality, like class, is just one window into the world. It does not explain everything and young activists should be discouraged from thinking so. Leaders on the left must work harder, not only to broaden the discussion and allow for diversity of opinion, but also to reconcile intersectionality with class politics in order that they work in tandem. Both must have equal billing going forward or they will become exclusionary.

Though undeniably well-intentioned, this latest vehicle to empowerment risks becoming yet another exclusive conversation about inclusivity, led by privileged groups, to the detriment of the people they claim to represent. It's hard to see how people in deprived communities can get excited about a form of politics that regards much of what they think, say and do as a form of abuse.

27

Frankenstein

THE LAST DAY of March 2017 marked the 16th anniversary of my mother's passing. Like every anniversary of her death, it passed without much fanfare. Other families devote time to celebrating the lives of those they've lost but in the case of my mum no such arrangement has ever been made. After her death, it was years before we even really understood what had happened. Communication between family members was so strained, for a variety of reasons, that her deteriorating health and eventual passing was not followed by closure. She doesn't even have a grave. There's nowhere to visit unless you fancy the three-hour drive to Fortrose, north of Inverness, where we unwisely scattered her ashes some years after she died. Up until that point, her remains were kept in an unglamorous urn, provided at very little cost by the crematorium, which was hidden away in the fireplace at my dad's, next to my brother's old bucket kit – a homemade device for smoking cannabis.

It's surprising what you pick up from your parents beyond the usual physical similarities. I still recall the Saturday afternoon in the spring of 2001 when she slipped away. It was the shriek of my sister that will stay with me. That blood-curdling cry when my granny re-emerged from the hall, where she'd been on the phone, and delivered the words we had been warned to expect at any moment:

'I'm sorry kids. Yer mammy's died.'

My gran never wore her heart on her sleeve. Raising two generations of a family while enduring the alcoholism and emotional abuse of my grandfather left her quite guarded about her feelings. But I detected the anguish in her eyes. Anguish she felt, and generally concealed, out of love for us. Almost before she had finished the sentence my sister leapt up from her chair, then convulsed in grief. The pain in her voice brought me out of shock and back into the room fully aware of what I'd just been told. She ran out of the room and collapsed in a heap on the stairs in emotional agony. My granny went out to try and console her.

I sat down on the chair closest to the window in a surreal state of disbelief. Much as I wanted to cry, or at least show some semblance of sorrow, the tears simply never came. My sister's reaction seemed so much more natural than mine and I became self-conscious that I wasn't expressing an adequate level of emotion for this situation. There had been so many times throughout my pained relationship with my mum that I had actively wished death upon her. Now my wish had been granted and here I was, cool and calm. I recall expressing a sense of relief that the whole sorry episode was finally over. Of course, the episode to which I referred was not my mother's slow decline in health but rather, the entire plot of her needlessly abbreviated life, a tragic story where I played a diminishing role; a recurring cameo as an angry son on the periphery of the long-running soap opera of her existence. An unremarkable drama-cum-farce that was cancelled abruptly after 36 predictable years. In just four years I will be older than she was when she died. Something about that fact really unsettles me. I used to worry I wouldn't even make it that far – and had good reason to. Thankfully, however, I am now one of five siblings who remain as fragile proof of her meandering existence.

Her short life and then her death sent ripples through all of us, ripples that became powerful waves, carrying with them the flotsam of past horrors we'd all start drinking to forget.

I remember holding court in the crematorium on the day of her funeral. The mourners were like my audience as I made jokes to pass the time before the service. We were stood in a glass house about a hundred yards from the church, waiting to be called in. I remember smugly thinking I had dodged a bullet because I wasn't really feeling that emotional. The mourners looked on wide-eyed as I captivated them with my observations and wisecracks. Suddenly their faces fell in eerie unison, eyelines shifting slightly to my left as if some terrible spectre had risen from the ground behind me. My urge to turn round was tempered by a fear of what I was about to see.

While I'd been relishing being the centre of attention, my mother's hearse had pulled up at my back to steal my thunder. I remember gasping for breath as my eyes filled with tears. It was real. She was gone and she was never coming back.

After the service, many of us gathered at a family member's house for the post-match analysis. People shared stories of my mum over a few drinks and I felt a strong sense that I had now become a man as my uncle handed me an ice-cold bottle of lager. There I stood in a black suit and tie, sporting a long dark coat, looking every inch the gentlemen. I was startled by the fact nobody questioned that I had just been given a bottle of booze despite only being 17 years old. Up until that point I had enjoyed a few drinking sessions but they usually ended with me getting bored or being violently sick. Never had I been permitted to consume alcohol around the family.

As I took the first few sips, it felt like the end of an era. My mum had cast such a long shadow over all of us. Now there was one less variable to worry about. The drink-induced nightmare we had been subjected to was finally over. It was the kind of moment that cold lager was brewed for. The relief spread from my lips and slowly across my face, down my arms and along each of my fingertips before resting in the pit of my stomach.

With the last remaining drops, everything came into soft focus.

What made this period doubly difficult was the fact that I had been estranged from my immediate relatives due to the family breakdown and was living between my friends and my grandparents. In the weeks and months following the funeral I had a lot of trouble sleeping. My granny's solution to this was to offer me a couple of tablets at night to help me drift off. They were called Co-Proxamol and she had been prescribed them by her doctor for pain relief. I can confirm they worked a treat.

28

Trainspotting

THE FIRST – AND only – time I watched *Trainspotting* was quite hazy due to the fact I was under the influence of a powerful opium-based sedative known as 'jellies'. My partner in crime – if I recall correctly – was keen to watch the film with me as he knew it was my first time seeing it. It's always a thrill to see someone else experience something you love for the very first time and this particular pal was by my side for a few of my 'firsts' – all of them drugs. He was now introducing me to the film that successfully captured not only the powerful effects of these drugs, but also the social conditions that created such high demand for them. Now and then I felt him glancing over to gauge my reaction at pivotal moments. But I doubt I gave him the response he was hoping for. The truth was, I could not enjoy the film because it was such a realistic depiction of drug-addled depravity that it brought memories of my own childhood flooding back.

The midday sun caught in the drapes, dust dancing in the beams breaking through the tears in the fabric, as they hung there lifeless over dirty windows. The room filled with an amber glow that gave the illusion of warmth. A belt tightening around a forearm before a syringe is plunged in. Most people will never witness such a thing let alone see their own mother do it. Most will instead ponder how people could allow themselves to become so bent out of shape that this kind of life could ever seem appealing. In fact, the best some of our commentariat could come up with at the time of *Trainspotting*'s release was a debate about whether it was too vulgar and whether it glamourised drugs. Talk about missing the point? But like many of the films and music videos that depict violence and drugs in hyper-realistic ways, *Trainspotting* provoked mixed feelings in me because it evoked my past. A past from which I was struggling to escape, sat there in my friend's house in an edgy euphoria, as the dawn raged against the back of those wonderful orange curtains.

The first time I took ecstasy was the first time in my life I had ever been free of fear. As the drug washed over me, cleansing me of resentment, anxiety and self-concern, all I can remember was being deeply preoccupied with the happiness of others. I had never felt so emotionally free, mentally agile and socially uninhibited. This was a peace I had never known. We talked, laughed, drank and smoked long into the night and when dawn broke, the adventure continued. My friend, who'd given me my first pill, was a purveyor of substances and as the morning kicked in he seemed to know exactly what we should do and, more to the point, what we should take. We returned to his house where we sipped on ice-cold beer, chain-smoked and listened to the audio of *Night of the Living Dead*. We imagined that we were the last two people alive in the zombie apocalypse and that the infected, swarming around outside, might break in at any moment and sink their teeth into our flesh. It never occurred to us at the time that we might be the ones coming down with something.

One of the reasons people become hooked on drugs so quickly is because coming off them is such a soul-destroying experience. And that's before you even become addicted. I'm not even talking about withdrawal symptoms. The term 'come-down' doesn't do it justice. 'Come-down' suggests there is something gentle or gradual about the experience. In truth, it's like breaking up in the atmosphere of a planet composed entirely of fear. Your 'come-down' is relative to the grandiosity of whichever delusion you were trying to sustain. Some people don't get bad come-downs because they are not running away from anything when they get high. For them, getting high is just an extension of their contentment. But for me, alcohol and drugs were a ticket out of my own head, an escape from a racing mind ravaged by anxiety, fear, resentment and insecurity. The hypervigilance that had helped me navigate my difficult childhood was now turning like a screw in the back of my waking mind, making it almost impossible for me to feel relaxed. Drugs relieved me of this burden. They soothed those difficult emotions. They did exactly what they were designed to do: they killed the pain. And they were so effective that life without them quickly became too difficult to bear. Before long, a life without drink or drugs was too abstract to contemplate.

I remember the very next week after my first ecstasy experience, being unable to settle as we waited in the corner of the nightclub for the dealer to arrive. The place felt empty and cold, the people aloof and distant. Some dealers are young and dweebish, others are hard and unhinged. But once you've developed a drug habit, none of that matters. You will go to whoever has the drugs, wherever they may be, no matter the risk. From the bleak high-rises of a Paisley housing scheme to the luxurious tenements of the West End, no hour was too late and no price was too much when we needed to get high. Recapturing that feeling of pure, unfiltered connection overrides all other concerns.

'What if he doesn't come? Where else will I get pills? How can I enjoy myself without them?' These became the questions preoccupying my every thought. Only a week before, I had tried ecstasy for the first time and felt like I was going to die of depression when I came down. But the second I recovered, all I wanted to do was get high again. It was as if my mind could not retain the memory of how horrible I felt afterwards, or the peripheral cost of going on a three-day bender. Without drugs, it was like the colour had been drained from the world. Without alcohol or drugs, I felt alone and afraid but when I knew they were on the way, or they were pumping through my system, the breaking dawn, a piece of music or a friend's unsolicited kindness would set my soul on fire. When you're high, you suddenly realise that all you ever have is the moment you are in. That nothing beyond that moment will ever exist. Contrary to many of the myths about drugs, they can have a profound, value-changing impact on a person's perception of themselves and the world. But that undeniable utility is, like all novelty, time-limited. There comes a point when there is nothing left of value to extract from the experience, when the drugs begin to insist on themselves regardless of how they make you feel. And as the reality you are running from gets more chaotic, and the delusions you are willing to entertain begin to deepen, you become isolated in the community of drinkers and users where such behaviour is acceptable. Things that would have shocked you in the past, whether it be lying to people or stealing money, become as routine as addiction and the dishonesty that feeds it leave you morally deformed.

I recall one dreary Sunday morning, walking with my friend on the obligatory off-sales run after a night of partying. Somehow, no matter how much alcohol I purchased the night before, I would always run out at about the same time in the morning. We shared a tin of lager and chain-smoked while deeply engrossed in conversation. Having been up all night taking MDMA, mushrooms and then ketamine, we decided to drop a jelly before leaving for the shop. I realised it was kicking in when I tripped, fell into some bins and started laughing. This family of drugs (opiates) was my personal favourite because they made me feel really mellow and chilled out, able to think clearly and express myself precisely the way I wanted to. The fire in my chest petered out, the butterflies in my stomach fluttered away and I became acutely aware of how every muscle in my body was tense and knotted. My entire posture completely changed when I was on these drugs. They gave me a sneaking glimpse of the kind of person I could be when I wasn't anxious or stressed. When I took these 'downers' I found it much easier to complete simple tasks like housework or running errands, things I'd normally procrastinate over because they filled me with anxiety. When I was on downers, I found it much easier to make phone calls and open letters. All the things I veered away from – or ignored completely – because they stressed me out, were a lot easier when I was high. I realised that I enjoyed being among people and that I wasn't as reclusive as I had believed. I also realised that opiates and alcohol were a nice mix.

But that Sunday morning was a good example of how a person can cross the threshold into a far more dangerous place, while still believing they are okay. Having just fallen into a bin, helped up by my friend, we were now waiting in a close, next to the off-sales, having arrived ten minutes early. We continued drinking and smoking, all the while believing ourselves to be upstanding members of the community. I think I even pissed in the close before we left. While we were all wrapped up in our fantasy of being two nonconformist renegades, valiantly swimming against a stream of wage slaves, we couldn't see that we were really the walking dead. We had no insight into what we had become. There we were, stood in someone else's property, having forced the door to gain access, talking loudly, smoking cigarettes and urinating, just to pass the time before getting our next cargo. Had I walked past people doing the exact same thing, my first reaction would be to judge them harshly and assume they were just junkies. But when it's you, there's surprisingly little awareness of the reality of what is going on. When you're stood there, you have a rich and textured context for yourself. It never occurs to you that you might be the junkie, or the ned or the selfish, dishonest, absentee brother and son. It's always someone else – never you.

The reality of my life was in stark contrast to the delusion I was entertaining. I had no job, had dropped out of education completely and was going weeks and months without contacting my family. I was on state benefits, preferring to delude myself that I had a mysterious mental illness when the majority of my problems were directly related to the fact I was a drunk and a drug addict. I was showing very little concern for anyone outside of my own narrow circle of drinkers and users and when my wee granny used to phone me, saying she was worried, I would get irritated and chastise her for interfering. Once I even accused her of taking her loneliness out on me. When it came to my friends, who never challenged my drinking – at least not at this point – then I had all the time in the world. But everyone else in my life was an afterthought, just like my responsibilities. My sense of victimhood closed me off from reality behind a wall of delusional self-justification. But had you told me that back then, I'd have gone through you faster than a bottle of Buckfast on an empty stomach. It was disorientating to confront the possibility that I was beginning to resemble everything I used to hate – so I didn't.

Instead, I burrowed deeper into the trenches of denial. At one point, I accidently smuggled drugs into a prison without even realising. The Valium, lodged in the lining of my trousers, wrapped in tinfoil, kept setting off the metal detector at the main gate. With a queue forming behind me, and unable to ascertain what was triggering the alarm, the guards let me through. On my walk into the prison, where I was due to work with young people with drug problems, I located the pills by sheer chance. But rather than shock or anxiety, or some semblance of self-awareness about the multiple dangers I was in, I felt a massive sense of relief and immediately ran to a toilet and took them all. Other times I would drink on the job, vanishing for five minutes here and there to take a swig of booze in a nearby toilet. Maybe that wouldn't be so bad if I was working in a warehouse, but most of my work was in the community with young people to whom I had a duty of care. The fact I couldn't see what a terrible example I was setting – and what a complete fraud I was – was perhaps a clue to the true depth of delusion one must entertain to continue feeding an addiction.

One day I received a call informing me that my granny had been rushed to hospital. I was working on a BBC programme – funnily enough, about young people binge-drinking. After work, I visited her in hospital and straight away I could see she was in a bad way. The next time I visited, I took a letter in which I had written my final goodbye to her. Nobody really knew what would happen but I had a feeling she didn't have long left. A few days later, we were told that she was going to be okay. Everyone was delighted with the news. But a few days before she was due to come home she contracted a hospital infection and became critically ill. Doctors advised the family to make their way to the hospital as soon as possible to say goodbye. But I didn't go. Despite the song and dance I had made only four years prior about not being able to hold my dying mother's hand one last time, here I was being given the option to sit by my granny's deathbed and say my piece. But I didn't go. This was the woman who practically raised me, but as she lay dying in a hospital ward, I was cowering at home, hiding behind a bottle, making excuses to explain why I could not attend. When the truth was, I didn't go because it would have meant I had to stop drinking for an hour.

That is the nightmare of addiction. And right at the core of it all was no longer simply pain or emotional trauma, as I often told myself, but a deep and malignant selfishness and lack of concern for the needs of others. An inability to see beyond my own pain, my own narrow worldview. Even my politics became no more than an extension of the personal resentments I used to justify my behaviour. I wouldn't get sober until I accepted that much of who I thought I was, including some of my deeply held convictions, were, in fact, self-serving and delusional – if they had even existed at all. Veering so close to self-destruction, I would have to become willing to confront the unthinkable idea that who I thought I was and what I believed about myself and the world, was false.

29

The Moral Landscape

WE LIKE TO take a lot of credit for our beliefs – even the ones we inherited that we did almost nothing to obtain. We wear those second-hand values like badges of honour, signalling to those around us that we are informed people of substance and principle, as opposed to that other sorry lot. That other lot, whose only function is providing the perfect absolute against which we, the enlightened, define ourselves. A slew of terms like 'loony lefty', 'Tory scum' or more recently slurs like 'social justice warrior' have become commonplace, deployed to reduce the groups with whom we disagree to a more manageable size. Dismissing challenges to our beliefs is as reflexive as blinking or breathing, because an unchallenged belief is easier to retain. Sticking to our guns, at the expense of all other considerations, appears to be the aim of the game.

But what if you are privately reconsidering your position on an issue? What if new information has come to light? What if some life experience has profoundly altered your perception or what if your interests realign? Maybe you've gone through an intellectual growth spurt having recently escaped the cannabis-scented smoke plume of your inebriated, cliché-ridden 20s? Maybe you've met a new partner or managed to escape the gravity of a toxic social circle? At various points in life, change becomes unavoidable. Where we exercise choice is in the extent to which we resist it. We all know what sticking to your principles looks like, but what about the process of coming to terms with the fact your beliefs have changed? That you are growing up and becoming a different person. Some people have children and others have near-death experiences. Some get offered a new job and others meet their soulmate. For me, getting sober, learning to stay sober and understanding why I was so unhappy has been a profound and life-altering process. So much so that it would probably take more effort to pretend that I haven't changed than it would to simply embrace all that is different. Though I'd be lying if I said I'm not aware that this has placed me at odds with many people I used to call friends or allies.

When going through such a fundamental shift in your thinking, everything in your life is on the table for review. Everything you think you are and everything you thought you used to be. This root and branch assessment, which I resisted stubbornly for years, was something I eventually had to submit to in order that I learn to live sober. And you can't truly know yourself without understanding what motivates your politics.

What I began to realise, as I peeled back the layers of pretension and self-justification laid down over a period of ten years, was that my political principles were not quite the beacon of selfless integrity and virtue I had long imagined they were. Quite the opposite in fact.

I'm sure I'm not just speaking for myself when I say that my left-wing beliefs were something I inherited, much like one inherits a title or a religion. While many of these beliefs have served me well and have benefits for wider society, had I been born and raised in a community where another ideology was prevalent, like Christianity or Conservatism, I'd likely have adopted that instead – and felt as strongly about it.

The fact that our beliefs are as much derived from blind chance as from choice or integrity doesn't stop us walking around with an unearned sense of moral superiority. Or is that just me? Difficult as it is to admit, if most of us really examine our beliefs beyond the platitudes we spout in public and read between the lines of our own hubris, we are likely to find several elements of pretention at play. Values we claim are for the benefit of others are often, conveniently, also for the benefit of ourselves. Take socialism, for example. Socialism, as far as I understand, is about providing a decent quality of life for everyone in society. But if I'm honest, that wasn't always my main motivation for being a socialist. Not really, if I genuinely examine my motives. Really, I just didn't like being poor. I felt excluded by society and culture, blamed the middle class and decided I wanted to rearrange society so that I wasn't at the bottom. I may have entertained the notion that it was about the wellbeing of other people but in the privacy of my own mind, it was about improving the conditions of my own life. It just so happened that there were lots of other people who wanted the same thing and our individual self-interest aligned, creating the comforting illusion we were engaging in collective altruism.

Yet I genuinely believed that because I was a socialist, this meant I was more moral and compassionate than, say, a social democrat or a libertarian. Essentially, I adopted the first set of beliefs I was exposed to and never bothered to investigate any further than my native ideological plantation.

Social media has given us a public platform to transmit our beliefs. Our threads and statuses, where we announce our opinions and condemn 'that other lot' are now logged and retrievable for all time. Everyone appears to be very sure of what they believe and that their beliefs are the right ones. But one thing you don't see a lot of on social media is people humbly announcing they were wrong about something, or that they have committed the cardinal sin of changing their mind and renouncing a false belief. The fact it's so rare to see people change their mind is probably why not that many of us do it. Or, at least, admit to doing it. We don't even know what such a process looks like, so entrenched in our worldview have we become. But secretly, haven't you ever pondered the rationale of the people you think are wrong? Haven't you ever felt that niggling doubt in the pit of your stomach, despite having just doubled-down on your unshakable political opinion? Haven't you ever been so wrong about something that you were subsequently compelled to consider, as a matter of urgency, what else you might be mistaken about?

In a global civilisation dogged by political and religious tribalism, occasionally asking ourselves where we may be mistaken becomes a radical political act. Isn't it a bit convenient that we, the 'good guys', always find ourselves not only on the right side of history but also on the right side of every argument on the right side of history? In an infinite universe, on a planet that has existed for billions of years, the chances of us being right about everything are slim, surely? That would be a bit of a coincidence, would it not? It's ludicrous when you really think about it. How could a person reasonably entertain such a yarn while believing themselves to be informed? You can't claim to have thought about anything at all if your own absurd nature doesn't cross your mind at least once a day. There's arguably more virtue in admitting you're mistaken and correcting your course, than there is in stubbornly believing you haven't been wrong since you were a teenager.

For all the integrity people ascribe to themselves for sticking to their guns, it's self-serving to take credit for hand-me-down beliefs, wearing them with a sense of pride all your life, regardless of how frayed or ugly they become. Just like my mother, who clung to the false belief that she could control and enjoy her drinking, even when she was diagnosed with a terminal illness, I too found it hard to see through the mirage of certain potent delusions. There was a time where I would have been deeply offended had anyone dared to suggest that the chaotic conditions of my life were partly of my own making; the radical idea that I, as a human being, had some responsibility for my own circumstances and that society, contrary to what I had always believed, was not to blame for all my problems.

30

The Metamorphosis

IN 1971, LEGENDARY Glaswegian shop steward Jimmy Reid famously told his co-workers occupying the United Clyde Shipbuilders: 'There will be no hooliganism. There will be no vandalism. There will be no bevvying... because the world is watching us.' This upset quite a few folk at the time. One of the workers said: 'We were all shocked when Jimmy said to us in front of a TV camera that there would be no hooliganism or bevvying because the world was watching us, which seemed to imply that we were hooligans and alcoholics to the very same world he spoke about.'

Reid risked offending a few people in order to address a specific truth: not all blame for our circumstances can be externalised; sometimes we're our own worst enemy. Reid was warning the workers not to conform to stereotypes and that if they wanted to achieve their objectives they had to take responsibility for their own behaviour – as well as railing against the system.

Taking responsibility is a hard thing to do. Especially when you believe it's someone else's job to pick up the slack. All my life I was told that the system was to blame for the problems in my family's life and that my family were to blame for the problems in mine. This belief that it was always someone else's fault was reinforced by the poverty industry and politicians who stood to gain from my willingness to defer to them.

I never got sober, at least for any length of time, until I admitted to myself that many of the predicaments in my adult life were of my own making. This, of course, is another taboo subject on the left. The idea of taking personal responsibility wherever you can

and that this is an important virtue in life is offensive to many.
I can't speak for everyone else who has experienced poverty, all
I can say is that my own life began to improve when I stopped
blaming other people for the things that were going wrong in it.
And nowhere did this apply more than in my emotional world,
where a lack of insight into what was really driving my stress,
sense of exclusion and ill health led me to adopting so many false
beliefs that I almost went completely insane. It's no wonder I was
so stressed out.

By now, I've hopefully established that one of the biggest
problems we face as a society is stress; how it shapes us as
individuals, families and communities; how it directs the thinking
that drives our behaviour and the things we do to manage it; and
how these coping strategies impact our families and communities.
Stress is the connective tissue between social problems such as
addiction, violence and chronic illness as well as the multiple
crises in our public services. I've argued that stress even plays a
part in shaping the tone and substance of political debate and
subsequent direction of society. In terms of poverty, stress is one
of the biggest variables in the equation. If we could significantly
reduce stress levels across society, we could raise the quality of
life for millions of people. Such is the sheer scale of the task, the
question that emerges is not so much 'How do we do it?' but
rather, 'Who is responsible for doing it?'

Who is best placed to manage our stress?

We need only sneak a glance at the low quality of dialogue
between the political parties to realise that, on the matter of
poverty (and many other issues), solutions will have to come
from us as individuals and communities. After all, is an issue as
important as our immediate wellbeing something we can really
afford to postpone until the government figures it out? Especially
when so much of it is within our own competence?

Remedying poverty is certainly not beyond us. When you
consider the advances in technology and medicine alone, it's silly
to place a ceiling on our ingenuity. But our collective stupidity is
similarly limitless, as are the configurations of complexity at play

in our relatively young civilisation. Eradicating poverty would require a global political consensus of the sort we have never seen. One day it will happen, but it's not going to be today. Or tomorrow. A pathological belief that only the state can resolve this issue is both disempowering and self-defeating in the short and medium term. This is not submission; this is to acknowledge the complexity of the matter. With the best will in the world, a problem like poverty will be around for centuries to come. The silver bullets we've been promised by our leaders are blanks.

Once you accept that the government isn't going to fix this issue any time soon, it whittles down the options. It removes some of the onus from government and places it directly on us. This should not mean a cessation of resistance or political activity, far from it. Choosing to confront the hard truth of these issues is streamlining things to make us more effective, both as individuals and as communities. But one thing we have to concede is that part of the solution lies with the individual.

It's counter-intuitive to accept responsibility for certain things, particularly when our circumstances are beyond our control. This is especially true if we have suffered abuse, neglect or oppression. But striving to take responsibility is not about blame, it's about honestly trying to identify what pieces of the puzzle are within our capacity to deal with. This approach is far more radical than simply attributing responsibility for every ill in society to a 'system' or a vaguely defined power dynamic – something we lefties have gotten all too good at. Aspiring to take responsibility is not about giving an unjust system a free pass, it's about recognising that we are part of that system and are, on some level, complicit in the dysfunction. For example, earlier I described the interplay with my emotional discomfort and a desire to consume junk food. How is such a problem most effectively traversed? What am I most likely to achieve sooner? Banning McDonald's or modifying my own lifestyle? McDonald's is supplying a demand from me and people like me, who are driven by our emotional needs. These emotional needs drive almost all of my activity as a consumer and citizen. Yes, businesses that are exploitative should be held to account for knowingly pushing harmful products on unsuspecting consumers. There are countless ethical dilemmas around the misinformation about food, deliberately promulgated in order to encourage the consumption of products known to have costly health outcomes. But if I am not willing to analyse my own role in the transaction and, as a conscious consumer, understand the societal implications of my choices, then my claim to be interested in change is disingenuous. My life is littered with examples of this. The prospect of looking for instances where you, and not someone else, or society, is at fault, may seem daunting (and deeply unfair), but if I cast a critical eye back through my own life, I can see countless instances where I was the biggest obstacle to my own progress. If I'm painfully honest with myself, a misguided sense of victimhood and the constant externalisation of blame blinded me to certain facts that would have helped me transcend my difficulties far sooner. It has to be asked, what quality of resistance to societal injustice was I actually bringing to the table, given the fact I lacked insight into even the most basic truths about my own life.

At the height of my drinking, my life was in a delicate balance between wilful delusion and procrastination. Sometimes it still is. There were so many areas where I could have taken some action but didn't, under the pretext that I couldn't or that someone or something else had to do it for me. Nowhere was this behaviour more evident than in relation to my mental health, which became the engine-room of my stress, delusion and atrocious lifestyle. I remember leaving doctors' surgeries with Valium prescriptions and going straight to the pub. I remember staggering into a pub rat-arsed and complaining to my girlfriend, who worked there, that addiction services were messing me around because I had to wait two weeks for an appointment. No surprise, I used that as a great excuse to keep drinking and missed the appointment the following fortnight. I used to tell myself that I drank because I had mental health problems and, throughout the course of my 20s, actively sought out a diagnosis to explain why I felt so low, so frightened and so depressed. I became so fixated with the idea

I was a sick person that I was blinded to the truth: I felt depressed because I was a delusional, selfish alcoholic. Waiting around for a mental health diagnosis probably added about five years to my destructive drinking.

This postponement of action and minimisation of the truth may seem inconsequential, but it said something about my willingness to turn a blind eye to my own hypocrisy. At this time in my life I was, perhaps, at my most strident and morally certain, but this sense of surety was completely unjustified and not only pushed me further from reality, while believing it firmly in my grasp, but also made my challenging circumstances more difficult. It added to my stress. So consumed by everything I thought was wrong with the world, I lost the capacity to be grateful.

After all, despite my apparent desire to see the fall of capitalism, this was a time when the system was bending over backwards to accommodate me.

I toured mental health services for years, genuinely believing I was either severely depressed or insane, when really, I was an exhausted, malnourished alcoholic, oscillating wildly between the high of inebriation and the crushing low of withdrawal and financial ruin. All the while I was demanding immediate change; rubbing my hands, awaiting the imminent collapse of society. My self-righteousness totally blinded me to the fact that the very society I was praying would fall, for all of its glaring flaws, was providing for my ever mutating needs. I had a slew of professionals on call, as well as accommodation, benefits and other forms of support. I had access to libraries full of knowledge and information about how to overcome many of the issues I faced as well as the internet where I could broaden the scope of my research. There were hundreds of free support groups all around the city, full of people who had got sober and remained so. Yet somehow, I was blind to all of this. These things didn't suit my narrative about society being bereft of integrity or compassion. Because I wasn't ready to honestly examine my problems which were, in the end, as much about my own attitudes and behaviour as they were about poverty or child abuse, I stubbornly continued a path of delusional self-obliteration.

It's absolutely correct to say I was mentally ill, but what I could not grasp was the extent of my sickness. Delusion had pervaded every corner of my mind. My once legitimate anger and grievance with aspects of my upbringing and with wider society became excuses to say and do whatever I wanted. I had lost all sense of perspective. I could only see where I had been harmed, never where I had harmed others. I could only see where I had been wronged, never where I had done wrong. And this was never challenged in left-wing circles, because everybody else was doing the exact same thing. People cheered me on, maniac that I was, not because what I was saying was true or useful, but because it validated the ones who were applauding. People who had been taught to believe that everything in the world had to change – but them.

At some point, I started believing the lie that I was not responsible for my own thoughts, feelings and actions. That these were all by-products of a system that mistreated and excluded me. And that I could only change and overcome these difficulties when society intervened in my circumstances or was dismantled and rebuilt.

It's this analysis of the role we as individuals play in shaping the conditions of our lives that is sorely missing from discussion on the left. If I read one more think-piece about how neo-liberal-ism is the root of all our problems, I might start drinking again. There is no question that the current economic system is riddled with contradiction, inequity and corruption. But in some sections of the left, you'd be forgiven for thinking all that was required was a quick coup d'état and the seemingly insoluble problems we face as individuals, families, communities and countries would disappear. By encouraging people to believe that their immediate problems are beyond their own expertise, the very agency poverty deprives them of is denied. Since my childhood, the left has pro-vided me with strong guiding principles and the foundations of my belief system. To this day, it's the activists on the radical left who are first responders to the bread and butter issues affecting society's most vulnerable; campaigning against zero hours con-tracts, raising awareness of the plight of the homeless or being prepared to physically fight skinheads and neo-Nazis. The left, at grassroots level, acts as our conscience. They annoy and irritate us with their appeals to our empathy. They exhaust and frustrate us with their chants and calls to action. And they call us out when we fall short. Many of the big concessions made by the powerful to the rest of us were only made possible by radicals who would not rest until something was done.

However, that does not absolve the left of complacency.

We also must acknowledge that these advances also took place within the very societies with which we so often find ourselves at odds. Surely, this is self-evident? Our system is riddled with internal contradiction, injustice and corruption, but is also very dynamic and offers a great many freedoms. For example, our current system, for all its flaws, is so dynamic that it can provide food, shelter and employment, as well as education, training and resources, for the very movements that are openly trying to overthrow it. This sort of liberty is not to be sneered at or taken for granted. Nor should we pretend that such freedom is easy to facilitate. Even when the new economic paradigm emerges, the leap we make as a civilisation will only have been possible because of the current system.

The emergence of the far right cannot be used as an excuse to turn a blind eye to some of the hypocrisies and indulgences in our politics. Nor can it be used to advocate a far-left radicalism that encourages closed-mindedness to other political ideas or a laissé faire attitude towards political violence. With so many absolutes against which we can now define ourselves, we must resist the temptation to project all blame for our personal and political circumstances onto bogey men and pantomime villains. We cannot hope to rebuild our communities, our movements or any viable society for that matter, without the ability to scrutinise and debate our own ideals. Not for the sake of navel-gazing but for the sake of establishing basic facts. There is no virtue in shooting down other people's bad ideas unless we occasionally turn the guns on our own, both as individuals and as movements. Scrutiny of our beliefs, motives and actions. Scrutiny of how our circumstances and self-interest subtly directs our thinking. And scrutiny of how we often believe in the legitimacy of our own fears and resentments, while mocking or dismissing those of others to whom we regard ourselves superior. I used to believe that anger alone, fuelled by a deep sense of unfairness about the conditions of my life, would be enough to change my circumstances for the better. But many of the conditions of my life began to change when I got less offended by the truth: some of my problems are mine to solve. The new frontier for individuals and movements who want to radically change society is to first recognise the need for radical change within ourselves.

The other good thing about examining your own attitudes and beliefs, and how they shape your experience and steer the direction of your life, is that you don't need an agency or a charity to parachute in and tell you what to do. It doesn't cost a penny and you can begin right away.

31

The Changeling

IN EARLY 2016 I found myself at the head of an angry mob. An acclaimed artist and activist named Ellie Harrison announced a new project on social media titled the Glasgow Effect, which drew derision from the public almost immediately. The aims and objectives were stated vaguely on a Facebook page where she'd chosen to use a picture of a bag of chips to capture, visually, the spirit of her year-long project. Unsurprisingly, many people took offence.

Harrison's project borrowed its title from a scientific study of the same name which attempted to explain why health statistics in Glasgow were worse than comparatively poor cities in the UK. In 2010, the Glasgow Centre for Population Health concluded that the deprivation profiles of Glasgow, Liverpool and Manchester were almost identical, but that premature deaths in Glasgow were over 30 per cent higher. And also that all deaths were around 15 per cent higher, across almost the entire population.

Glasgow's mortality rates are the highest in the UK and among the highest in Europe. With a population of over a million, life expectancy is 71.6 years for men and 78 years for women – around seven and four years, respectively, below the national average. In 2008, the World Health Organisation estimated that the life expectancy for men in the Calton area of Glasgow was just 54 years. To put that in some context, had I been born in the Calton, then at 33, I've already lived more than half my life; marked for death more than ten years before my retirement age.

When the study was published, the Glasgow Effect became shorthand for poverty. The pertinent finding being a link between the early years brain development of children living in poverty and the health conditions and precarious circumstances that often plague them later in life. The report found that 'chronically activated stress responses, especially in children, affect the structure of parts of the frontal lobes of the brain, and that these determine the physical reaction to stress, which could result in chronic ill health'. Chief Medical Officer Harry Burns also suggested that the ability to attain good health depended, in part, on whether people felt in control of their lives, and whether they see their environments as threatening or supportive.

For those of us affected by this phenomenon, the Glasgow Effect was proof that we were not insane or paranoid – at least not completely. Proof that while we must take personal responsibility for our actions, that the social conditions we are exposed to have a lot to answer for. The Glasgow Effect eloquently described, in scientific terms, the reality of our existence; going about our days, oblivious to the social and psychological disadvantages that define our chaotic and abbreviated lives. It described why social mobility was so low, why opportunity was so scarce and how living in conditions of chronic stress had inhibited, impaired and deformed us.

Ellie Harrison's year-long contemporary art project, symbolised by a greasy bag of chips, seemed to mock the seriousness and complexity of this issue.

Harrison's project, though she didn't make it very clear at the time, was an attempt to investigate how being restricted to one geographical area for a year, in this case Glasgow, impacted on her ability to live and work as a professional artist. Throughout the year, she would document and reflect on how this limitation affected everything, from her social life, identity and mental health to her employability and even her carbon footprint. The project reflected Ellie's personal interests as an activist, artist and citizen living in Scotland. Interests which, while legitimate, were sadly not shared by many of Glasgow's poorer residents, for whom the Glasgow Effect was not merely a concept but an oppressive matrix of overlapping inequalities. Ellie's cause was not helped by the fact that she chose to use academic language in the vague description of her project, which naturally aroused prejudice among those who had grown wary of jargon – because they associate it with political exclusion and exploitation.

On a Facebook page, created for the project, Ellie wrote:

The Glasgow Effect is a year-long 'action research' project/ durational performance, for which artist Ellie Harrison will not travel outside Greater Glasgow for a whole year (except in the event of the ill health / death of close relative or friend).

By setting this one simple restriction to her current lifestyle, she intends to test the limits of a 'sustainable practice' and to challenge the demand-to-travel placed upon the 'successful' artist / academic. The experiment will enable her to cut her carbon footprint and increase her sense of belonging, by encouraging her to seek out and create 'local opportunities' testing what becomes possible when she invests all her ideas, time and energy within the city where she lives.

This short description, without even intending it, was encoded with everything people from deprived communities have grown sceptical of over the years. Culture, participation, the arts; all these things that people claim are accessible but which always appear to be the exclusive preserve of those who use phrases like 'action research project' and 'sustainable practice' – high status language that sets alarm bells ringing. Then there was the money. Not only was Ellie being paid £15,000 to spend a year analysing the plight of the 'successful artist', she was going to benevolently 'create local opportunities'. Her concerns, pertinent as they might have been, were not shared in those communities where people have little time or headspace to consider carbon footprints or the personal sacrifice of successful contemporary artists. This clumsy initial approach, rooted in a deep lack of understanding of the cultural dynamics at play in the city, fertilised a social media storm that very quickly got out of hand.

The consensus was that 'some artist' 'from England' 'was being paid 15 grand' to 'live in Glasgow for a year' to see how being stuck in one geographical location affected her ability to work. To be honest, the consensus was not inaccurate, despite many claims to the contrary. People rightly felt offended that someone was being paid £15,000 to simulate being stuck in Glasgow when so many people really were stuck in Glasgow. The premise of the project appeared to mock those who were not as socially mobile as people like Ellie, a university lecturer as well as a professional artist, by attempting to mimic the painful reality of many Glaswegian lives.

For many people, the Glasgow Effect was a symbol of class inequality, expressed in myriad ways. To Ellie and her supporters – and funders – the Glasgow Effect was a catchphrase, gentrified and reappropriated for a contemporary arts project, illustrated by a soggy bag of deep-fried food. Had such a brazen misunderstanding occurred about any other group in society, the very people applauding Ellie would have been crying foul; accusing people of revictimising the marginalised, of triggering people, of reifying the interdependent structural oppressions of capitalism or patriarchy. But none of that mattered in this instance. Or at least, that's how it seemed.

So it fell to me to try and set them all straight. I decided to do that by going for Ellie directly, vindicated by the many online supporters willing me on to represent the plight of the working class. I wouldn't settle until everyone understood why her project was misguided. Why it was offensive. And why they had to reconsider their position if they genuinely couldn't see that. I wouldn't stop until I had proved my point. My first course of action was to publish a strongly worded piece in which I made the case that public anger at Harrison's project was justified and that it was, primarily, rooted in anger about class disparity:

Shake yourselves awake. This was never about attacking one unfortunately titled project.

If only influential sections of the arts community were as insightful and articulate as they seem to think they are. If only they could grasp the fact people are not actually annoyed at Ellie or even conceptual art. If only they could grapple with the thorny reality that people are actually annoyed at the big floppy-haired elephant in the green room: they are annoyed at rising social inequality and how this expresses itself culturally.

We have to get honest with ourselves about where scepticism of certain forms of art and culture comes from. It comes from the fact we are living in two different worlds.

In working class communities, symbols of culture and identity are ripped out, renamed, sold off, mysteriously burned down or demolished – in the name of progress.

So, when Creative Scotland decides to bankroll one artist's investigation into how being stuck in Glasgow with no road out affects your social life, career and mental health then you better f***ing believe some Glaswegians are going to be fuming about it.

The piece was widely read and within 24 hours had generated some responses. I was soon approached for comment by the *Daily Record* and I obliged, sensing an opportunity to spin the controversy into a debate about class. I took some time to consider how best to reframe Ellie's project.

The next day I gave the following statement: 'There are thousands of artists who articulate what living in poverty is like. These artists are often marginalised. A recent study in the *Guardian* showed the arts is dominated by middle class people. Ellie's project epitomises that. It's horrendously crass to parachute someone in on a poverty safari.'

And there it was: 'Poverty Safari'. Many people scratched their heads, wondering what I meant by the phrase. When I intervened in the debate, I was trying to articulate what I felt the public anger was about. My aim was to lend some context to it, as I could see that much of it was being lost in translation and misunderstood.

This was an issue I'd been struggling to express, having gained a modest public platform in an arts and media culture dominated by liberal, middle class perspectives. I was used to having things explained to me whenever I piped up with an opinion, so I felt this was the perfect time for everyone to sit down and have this stuff explained to them for a change. I saw it as my responsibility to try and act as a translator between the classes, making sure that everyone understood that Ellie's project was not solely what people were upset about. That much of this anger was a convergence of disparate themes – early years, education, lifestyle, deprivation, social mobility and political exclusion. That unfortunately for Ellie, she came to epitomise what many people believed the real issue was: class. Unsurprisingly, I was soon shut down by the commentariat and influential sections of the arts; by people who'd been cut into the action in some way.

The uproar from sections of the public about Ellie Harrison's project – and scepticism of politics, arts, media and culture, generally – must be seen in this broader context to be truly understood. For the people who were angry about it, this was just another example of their needs and aspirations being ignored, stepped over, vilified, sneered at or exploited. When I came up with the phrase 'Poverty Safari' it was not simply a cheap swipe at Ellie's project, it was an attempt to distil everything I had learned in my experience as a working class person, attempting to escape poverty whilst traversing these wildly different cultural domains. 'Poverty Safari' was an attempt to hold a mirror up to Ellie's good intentions and show exactly why they were doomed to be misinterpreted. 'Poverty Safari' was my answer to the question: 'Why are you so angry?'

But even that was regarded by many as either misguided or offensive.

However, that was not the whole story. As is usually the case, there was something else at play which had conveniently escaped my notice as I threw myself headfirst into the cauldron of a national debate. While many of my arguments were correct and I had successfully expressed the thoughts and feelings of many people who were being written off as angry and abusive, my motives for getting involved were less clear. My entire posture towards Ellie's project, while orientated by my lifelong interest in the topic of social inequality, was also shaped by my assumptions and prejudices about Ellie herself – as a middle class person. I was viewing her through my class lens. In truth, all I knew about her project was what I had heard on social media. If I'm completely honest, I only got involved because there was an expectation that I should. '£15,000 to live in Glasgow for a year? Outrageous. I wonder what Loki will have to say about this?' This social expectation that I should be the one to involve myself was what had catalysed my intervention. The stage was set for me to say something, so I did, but I hadn't stopped to really consider what was going on. Really, deep down, I saw the opportunity to use Ellie as a way of lashing out at something else. The backlash from her project had created such a controversy that the conversation was becoming global, and, perhaps unconsciously, a part of me resented the prominence her project was receiving. A part of me was angry, jealous even, that hers should be the one at the heart of so much interest, debate and discussion. To me, the issues her project was concerned with were detached, indulgent and exclusive; the fact so many people were arguing about them seemed like a terrible waste.

But as the days passed, I began to reflect more deeply on my reasons for getting involved. What emerged was quite startling for me. Beneath all the rhetoric about class, and the insight about cultural inequality and social mobility, ran a river of pure resentment which coursed through me like a drug. This resentment, to which I was either blind or believed legitimate, had clouded my mind precisely at a moment when I believed I was thinking most clearly. This is to say, I acted believing I was motivated by one thing when, in truth, it was about something else entirely. My impulse was attack, pounce, maim and devour, without attempting to comprehend even the most basic facts on the matter. This impulse was so strong, and stimulated such a potent sense of righteousness, that there was absolutely no doubt

in my mind that I was justified to go after Ellie. There was no
doubt that Ellie's project had to be taken down and that she, as
an artist, had to be discredited in some way.

There are certainly circumstances where this approach may
have been appropriate but what became apparent to me later was
that I was acting out of revenge. Not against Ellie, who I had
never met, but against something more vague, elusive and inde-
finable. Deep down beneath the almost arrogant veneer, I felt so
powerless that the opportunity to land one on a perceived enemy
was impossible to resist – even if it meant being petty or disingenuous. What I had turned a blind eye to, when the opportunity to
insert myself into the conversation arose, was that I had dehu-
manised Ellie, reducing her to a caricature and therefore easy to
dismiss. Her 'middle classness' became a way to whittle her and
her supporters down to a more manageable size, so that I could
retain a comforting false belief. I retrofitted Ellie with a middle
class identity, despite not knowing anything about her, and then
used that as a justification for trying to derail her project. But,
easy and tempting as it was to hide behind the common left-wing
trope of 'punching up', in the pit of my stomach I knew, regardless of the validity of my argument, that I had adopted it under
false pretences. This wasn't about class, or cultural inequality, at
least not in the way I thought it was. This was about striking back
and hurting the people I believed were excluding me. The problem
here was that, while Ellie appeared to fit the profile of an oppres-
sor in my head, in reality she was nothing of the sort. Therefore,
whatever legitimate grievance I had with her project was severely
undermined by the manner in which I attempted to air it out.

When the opportunity to engage an international debate about
class presented itself, I sabotaged it to settle a score, while draping
myself in the veil of an activist. And it wasn't the first time. (Since
then, I've been on the receiving end of this kind of anger and,
ironically, the first words that came out of my mouth when the
lynch mob darkened my digital doorway were 'Please, calm
down.') Much as I hate to admit it, I should have taken some time
to properly consider the best way to respond to Ellie's project. I'd

been raised to think that any anger I felt was legitimate, merely by virtue of the fact I was lower class. But even if this were true, the anger itself was only useful when expressed at the correct moment, in the correct way. It's only legitimate when it's deployed with the right quality of intention and even then, its utility is time-limited. Just like the booze, the fags, the drugs and the junk food, the novelty of righteous anger soon wears off, leaving you only with a compulsion to get hot and bothered, when often the solution to the problem is staring you straight in the face. This isn't a popular thing to say on the left, but it's an honest one. In this case, I had used righteous anger as a smokescreen to conceal something more self-serving. I had used the 'working class' as a Trojan horse to advance my own personal agenda. And I did all of this while believing myself to be well informed and deeply virtuous, unaware of how personal resentment was subtly directing my thinking.

I am sure you have no idea what I'm talking about.

Had I looked a little further into Ellie's project, I would have found many areas of common ground between us. Ellie was a renowned social activist with a keen interest in the renationalisation of buses – hardly a hot topic for the chattering classes. And while her environmental concerns may have appeared detached or indulgent to me at first, the truth was, Ellie's politics were almost identical to those of the Pollok Free State, a group I'd been harping on about since my teens because I regarded it as the epitome of community ethics. As I began to consider her work more deeply, what I found was someone with deep principles about social equality, political participation and the environment. These were not simply pretensions she harboured or platitudes she spoke in, but principles she had chosen to live by that were reflected in every aspect of her life. From her diet, to her chosen modes of transportation, to recycling and in her own art and career, Ellie had striven to live in alignment with her values, which were about taking responsibility for how we live in the world. I started to see her in a new light, grudgingly at first, but as I let go of my false beliefs it made some room for new insights to emerge.

These irritating tropes of middle class life, around veganism, cycling and healthy eating, really served a practical function and were not necessarily as pretentious as I thought. As well as being markedly cheaper, many of these seemingly indulgent lifestyle choices were about living in accordance with the needs of the wider community, the environment and devising a sustainable lifestyle that integrated those needs. Trends and products that I thought were for posh people and hipsters were often about practical, healthy, more environmentally friendly alternatives to products and lifestyle choices that were counter-productive, or unethical in some way. Ellie's attention to detail, her aspiration to live an ethical life, for the benefit of everyone, were manifest in her Glasgow Effect project. She was actively trying to find out if it was possible for a working artist to remain in one city for a year, devoting her time to a single community, while reducing the environmental impact of her day-to-day existence.

In many ways, her investigation was the practical extension of my own investigation into poverty. But where I was keen to understand the context of what came before, whether it be the housing schemes or my own upbringing, she was articulating what might come next. She was beginning to reimagine the society that had left so many in my community feeling excluded, apathetic and chronically ill. But I didn't give myself a chance to see all that. I wasn't open to that possibility. My urge for retribution was so strong that it blinded me to the fact we were fighting for the same thing. When I realised the depth of my error, it reframed my whole perception of class and, to some extent, of poverty. Having conceded my approach had been misguided, I was then forced to ponder what else I might be wrong about. And surprise surprise, when my attitude became less adversarial, the people who didn't see eye-to-eye with me in the beginning became far more willing to concede where they were at fault too.

Rather than allowing the facts of the matter to be held hostage by false belief and personal bias, informed by a cascade of self-delusion, prejudice and lingering resentment masquerading as communitarian concern, I simply held my hands up and said: 'I'm sorry. I was wrong.' Instead of attempting to reorder reality around my own petty emotional impulses while presenting myself as a virtuous and rational observer, I decided to turn my critical eye inward.

Who'd have thought that, believing myself to be of clear mind, I was behaving vindictively? Who would have known that my desire to bring clarity to an issue was really obscuring my view of it? And this wasn't just any issue. This was an issue that was fundamental to my own development as a human being. This was an issue that I specialised in and that had come to define my life. Yet here I was, on a wild goose chase of my own making, believing myself to be firmly in the driver's seat. Such a lack of insight into my own nature undermined any claim I had to know anything at all, let alone how to understand and solve the complex litany of problems facing our society.

Perhaps none of this seems relevant to a discussion about poverty. Perhaps, when you identify as a 'poor person' or some other form of injured party or oppressed or marginalised group, then you shouldn't be expected to scrutinise your own thinking and behaviour. But it strikes me that much of my thinking and reasoning throughout the years has been peppered with similar hypocrisy. Hypocrisy, where I absolved myself of responsibility for behaving the same way as those I criticised, while wondering why dialogue was so frustrating and disheartening. At the root of my motivation, in this intervention, lay a deep resentment about class. A resentment that was validated and legitimised by my politics – politics which I had inherited by pure chance and weaponised at the earliest opportunity as an extension of my own personal resentments.

Again, I'm sure you have no idea what I'm talking about.

A few weeks after the Glasgow Effect scandal died down, I was invited to take part in a panel discussion with Ellie. When I arrived at the venue I immediately noticed her at the front door wearing a lollipop lady's jacket. The air of pretension I assumed she would emit was actually an air of self-deprecation; she clearly didn't take herself as seriously as I took myself. My heart rate quickened, as I had been anticipating the moment we would first

speak and suddenly found myself thrust into her path unexpect-
edly. Fortunately, she was swamped by fans keen to hear about
her experience, so I made my way into the venue, having dodged
a bullet, and composed myself. It was my intention to apologise
to Ellie before the public discussion took place, but now in the
venue, it was too busy to give it the attention it deserved.

I sat down with a friend who'd written one of the many
responses to my intervention that had forced me to reflect on my
actions. To my right, Ellie was meeting and greeting friends and
audience members. Being in the room with her, I could now get a
sense of the immense strain Ellie had clearly been under since the
outrage earlier in the year. She looked nervous, shell-shocked and
exhausted. The reality of what it must be like to be the one the
social media hounds are chasing began to hit me; Ellie had been
through a horrendous personal ordeal. The backlash had lasted
for weeks, made worse by the fact her funders and employers had
to get involved to clarify publicly certain details about her job and
application. This had led to even more scrutiny and speculation
of her personal life. Ellie had not only been on the receiving end
of robust mainstream media criticism, but scrolls and scrolls of
vile, misogynistic hate-filled vitriol. Everything from her career to
her personal appearance and sexuality had become fair game, as
thousands of armchair critics joined the pile-on – a pile-on I had
helped to create. As I sat there, rather awkwardly, reflecting on
my part in all of this, another of Ellie's friends arrived.

They hugged, the embrace lasting a little longer than a simple
hello. I wondered if perhaps they been reunited after a long period
of time or that maybe this was the first time they'd crossed paths
since Ellie became public enemy number one?

Then, despite the noise all around me, I heard gentle sobbing.
Out of the corner of my eye, I saw Ellie's head rise and fall as she
leaned into her friend's chest. When confronted with the reality
of this woman, as opposed to the caricature I had created, it was
a little harder to retain the beliefs I had entertained previously.
Here was a decent, fragile human being who had acted with good
intentions, sobbing her heart out. A woman who was almost

broken. The self-justification about class, culture and 'punching-up' suddenly felt hollow, self-serving and delusional. Yes, her approach was misguided, clumsy and poorly conceived. Yes, her assumptions about life in working class communities deserved to be challenged. Yes, there were important questions that had to be answered about why so many people felt politically excluded and culturally misrepresented and sometimes anger and rage was justified – even necessary. But as she wiped her eyes, and I pretended not to notice, it suddenly became apparent how destructive my class politics had really become. I was so consumed by my own anger and moral certainty, it had blinded me to the fact that Ellie Harrison, in all her middle class glory, was not an enemy, but an ally in the war I'd been fighting all my life. It then occurred to me, grudgingly, that should I ever feel like 'punching-up' again in future, I might want to double-check who I'm hitting first.

32

Rules For Radicals

'IT'S NOT THAT we have a short time to live but that we waste much of it', wrote the Stoic, Seneca, nearly 2,000 years ago, in what proved to be a prescient chin-stroking session in Ancient Rome. One suspects he was not the first person to ponder the dilemma of how best to live a life but I'm sure we're all glad he managed to jot the thought down before forgetting it. It's immensely comforting to know that even back then, when human life was considerably briefer – around 40 years – that people were still pissing away perfectly serviceable afternoons considering the intractable problems of their existence. I wonder what Seneca would have said had he known that two millennia later, with twice the time on our hands, that we'd still be none the wiser.

As a by-product of this ruminating, thinkers like Seneca created much of the intellectual scaffolding on which many of our own thoughts and opinions hang; the layers and levels of understanding, the gradient at which we enter discussions and the trajectory of our inquiries through them. These habits of thinking did not always come as naturally as they seem to. They were achieved through difficult debate, much of it provoking outrage and discomfort, that subsequently produced a vast, patchwork map for living. A map with which we've become so accustomed we now view merely as cliché.

Think of every unremarkable proverb you know and reimagine it being uttered for the first time. We take these little nuggets of wisdom for granted. But like many of the beliefs we attribute to our own virtue, we did almost nothing to obtain them. Proverbs, and most of the other knowledge we trade as currency, are the product of someone else's leg-work. We are all copycats, frauds and tricksters, lying about the books we've read. Our wandering minds are full of memes uploaded by the people who came before us, to whom we rarely give credit or pay tribute, unless it's to signal our own intelligence. But these truths, distilled by others and later reclaimed by us mere mortals, attempt to cut to the heart of the matter by tearing through the hubris of the era, with little regard for the pretensions of the day. And there are few clichés as simple or ubiquitous as 'life's too short' which, it would appear, is what Seneca the Younger was grappling with in his essay 'The Shortness of Life'.

'Life is long enough,' he wrote, 'and it's been given to us in generous measure for accomplishing the greatest things, if the whole of it is well invested. But when life is squandered through soft and careless living, and when it's spent on no worthwhile pursuit, death finally presses and we realise that the life which we didn't notice passing has passed away.'

Much of my own life has been squandered in years of careless or misdirected thinking. The replaying of old arguments and perceived victories, the simulation of rich fantasies that go beyond the mundane and into the absurd or extreme. Too much of this, for too long, made me deeply unhappy. Unable to ascertain why, I adopted false beliefs that appeared to explain it.

I'd cast my mind over the past, believing I was trying to uncover the truth of the matter, but my real intention, when conducting this pretence at inquiry, was rarely to find the truth, or to locate my own part in some conflict or confusion; rather, my intent was always to absolve myself of blame – while generously apportioning it to others. If only I had given the people I resented as much leeway as I was willing to give myself, what then? Perhaps it's natural to cast yourself as the protagonist of your own story. To only see life from your own perspective. But, just because it's natural does not mean it's right. Even now, I am still clearing up the wreckage of a life that was based on little else other than doing whatever felt good at the time. I chose to ignore the wisdom of those who came before me and I paid a heavy price.

For many people, nothing is more frustrating or perplexing than the wisdom of their own parents. But those days are now in the past and my relationship with my father has improved over the years as I've grown. Time is a great healer, to use another wonderful cliché, and is often helped along when a little distance is thrown in for good measure. When stress tears your family apart, setting everyone on their own little collision course with life, then sometimes the only thing you can do is get out of one another's way. In doing so, you create an opportunity for reflection and growth and, in the case of my dad and me, a bit of physical distance has created the potential for compassion and understanding.

Life seems to click back into place when harmony breaks out between the warring factions of a family. You realise the futility of fighting and learn to avoid it. For some, that means biting their tongue, for others, only visiting occasionally. And while it isn't always easy, sometimes the only solution is to forgive and forget. Anything less will make you ill, no matter how justified you are in your anger. It's usually the case that those who wronged us were, themselves, wronged at some point too, just as it's likely that those of us who have been harmed by others will repay the favour countless times throughout the course of our lives. We are all, to some extent, victims and abusers at different stages of our lives, but we tend only to recall those times when we were harmed. That might be natural, but it's not always the truth.

In the case of my mother, she didn't have much of a chance. Having been raped at a young age and rejected by her mother for revealing it, she pursued connection through sex, alcohol, drugs and, later, children. But every attempt at connection failed along with her coping strategies. As her parents succumbed to their own addictions and her narrowing circle of friends and siblings either moved on with their lives, got sober or died with needles in their arms, she grew more isolated from reality. My mum never got the chance to gain insight into how abnormal her life was; that there was another way of thinking and of being. She never had anything else to compare it to. Just as I felt self-conscious and anxious whenever I mixed with people I perceived as higher class than me, she recoiled from the most basic human interactions unless she was intoxicated. Even from her own children. That's how low an opinion she had of herself. In my mother's eyes, where I once saw only hatred I now see pain, trauma and a deep frustration at longing to feel connected but not knowing how. In her eyes, I see myself. In her short life, I see my alternative future, should I be tempted back into that world of smoke and mirrors. The older I get, the more I begin to appreciate how hard it must have been for my parents, kids themselves when I was born, and in their clichés I now see kernels of wisdom.

As I continue to recover from the past and become adjusted to life's often less than ideal rhythms, the old resentments, rooted in youthful ideals, have made way for a new pragmatism. This tendency away from self-centeredness and desire to set the past aside is not completely altruistic, despite being beneficial to others. It's based on an uncomfortable truth: the longer I'm alive, the higher likelihood there is of making similar missteps to those I've spent much of my life resentfully condemning.

As a child, I condemned my mother's drinking and hated her for being an absent member of our family. But by my teens, I was incapable of being around family unless I was drunk. I couldn't understand how she could leave us and not wonder how we were or what we were doing. But by the time I started drinking, I rarely took an interest in the lives of my siblings unless they came to one of my parties. Of course, like all of my misgivings and indiscretions, it was always different when *I* did it. There was always some twist of reasoning, some acrobatic feat of self-justification that meant I didn't have to forsake my permanent place on the moral high ground, but deep down I always knew I was a hypocrite and a fraud and a liar. I've learned to temper and examine my indignation at other people's behaviour, particularly my parents', because my experience tells me I am doomed to repeat the things I once condemned – if I'm not careful.

As it happens, much of the world view I am now beginning to claim as my own really came from my dad; my values, attitudes and beliefs as well as my flaws, pet peeves and eccentricities. At some point in my life – probably when I was kicked out before my mum died – I began to view my dad as the villain of my story. But that was merely part of the delusion. I was ungrateful, and hadn't matured enough to acknowledge this. Evidence of my dishonest thinking can be found in my willingness to attribute my failures and problems to my parents, while taking sole credit for any successes I may have had, and the rather juvenile idea that should I break free from the gravity of poverty, it would be in spite of my mother and father, rather than because of them.

I believe I then mapped this delusion onto society itself.

My arrogance and naivety blinded me to the fact that my father's influence was all-pervasive in my life – right down to the fact I chose to become an artist. Like the thinkers of the Ancient World, who did all the heavy lifting for us, I minimised and discarded my father's wisdom as outdated and unfashionable when, in truth, it provided me with the firmest possible footing. Within a year of leaving home and finding myself able to indulge in the things my dad had placed strict limitations on, such as drinking, junk food and cigarettes, my life had spun hopelessly out of control.

My dad always placed an emphasis on taking responsibility financially and respecting people's wishes and property. But as soon as I was out the door, I became an irresponsible, impulsive confusion of mounting excess. He did his best to encourage me to eat well and exercise regularly, making sure we all had working bicycles and taking us all swimming once a week. Above all, he always said that I should never, under any circumstances, settle for a job I didn't like if I had dreams of being a writer.

The virtues he tried to instil in me would probably have saved me many years of misery and stress had I been wise enough to live by them sooner. But I vilified him, omitting his wisdom from my thinking completely, choosing instead to absorb the wisdom of fairweather friends and manipulative drinking buddies, who told me whatever half-truths I wanted to hear. I shudder to think how little I knew, precisely at those moments when I thought I knew it all, and how vulnerable such a lack of insight really made me. Which is why I doubt I'll ever be truly certain of anything again

– perhaps other than my own capacity to be stunningly wrong.

Today is the day I finally finish this book. If I'd known writing it was going to be so hard, I'd have stuck to just trying to read one. It's mid-morning and I'm sitting in Starbucks, overlooking the foyer at the Silverburn, nearly nine years to the day since it opened. It's safe to say, this isn't where I imagined I'd be when I started on this journey. For years, I've been rolling my eyes at the mention of this place and throwing up middle fingers whenever I passed it. The Silverburn, like so many other things, became an icon that seemed to encapsulate everything that was wrong with my world. But things change and so have I. Sometimes I worry that I'm not changing for the better. That I've grown too distant from my roots or that I am being absorbed by the very system I've spent my life railing against. Other times, I feel I had no choice but to change and that the problem, if there is one, lies with those who've insisted on remaining the same despite all that has transpired. I guess I'll never really know if this change I'm going through is because I have forsaken my principles or because I've gained a deeper insight into life and moved forward as a result. Whichever it is, thankfully I no longer have time to ponder such matters.

Next to me stands a bright orange buggy, with its hood pulled up. Tucked inside, purring loudly, deep in his mid-morning nap, is a one-year-old boy called Daniel. He is my son. It was on the first day of an honest attempt to stop smoking that I received news I would become a father in the spring of 2016. The news was particularly frightening, not least because I had spent my 20s privately pondering just how bad a father I would be should a child have the misfortune of finding itself under my wing. For years, negative self-talk convinced me that I was unfit to be a parent. In fact, I internalised the rather grandiose notion that my greatest gift to the world would be to never reproduce, thus withholding my DNA, which I'd long considered defective. Deep down, my biggest fear about becoming a father was that I might pass my false beliefs onto my child, plaguing his life with needless pain, conflict and disorientating self-doubt. When he was born he didn't look like a baby. I remember what resembled a small purple alien, contained in a see-through bag. My only experience of childbirth up until that point was watching medical dramas as a kid, my grandparents awkwardly coughing over the bits where doctors referred to 'vaginas'. For this reason, I expected my son to arrive fully formed in a high chair wearing a *Jungle Book* onesie. The reality was far more startling. There was a lot of blood and my partner was both delirious with pain and fully aware the baby wasn't making any noise. Those first few seconds of silence were the longest, as I began to physically convulse at the thought something might be wrong.

And then he cried. His baby skin turned from purple to pink, his eyes slowly opened and out of a tiny mouth rang the top of his little lungs. I never knew I'd be so relieved to hear a baby screaming. The novelty wore off pretty quickly. One year later, and everything in my life has changed. Not necessarily because I wanted it to, but because it had to. The old way didn't work. Today, I realise that the best contribution I can make to society is to raise a healthy, happy and secure child. Today, I realise that the most practical way of transforming my community is to first transform myself and, having done so, find a way to express how I did that to as many people as possible.

Some will argue that this introspection is merely another form of structural oppression; an extension of neo-liberal economics that encourages individuals to avert their eyes from the injustice of the world and, instead, focus on self-improvement. Others will argue that it's a cop-out because it doesn't challenge power. To them I say this: you are no use to any family, community, cause or movement unless you are first able to manage, maintain and operate the machinery of your own life. These are the means of production that one must first seize before meaningful change can occur. This doesn't mean resistance has to stop. Nor does it mean power, corruption and injustice shouldn't be challenged, it simply means that running parallel to all of that necessary action must be a willingness to subject one's own thinking and behaviour to a similar quality of scrutiny. That's not a cop out; that's radicalism in the 21st century.

I made every excuse, blamed every scapegoat and denied every truth. But as it happens, the great theme of my life was not poverty, as I had always imagined, but the false beliefs I unconsciously adopted to survive it; the myths I internalised to conceal the true nature of many of my problems. It hadn't occurred to me that a root-and-branch analysis of poverty might involve asking some searching and difficult questions of myself too. For some reason, despite my apparent concern that this issue be scrutinised forensically, I conveniently exempted myself from the analysis while placing everything else under a microscope. I had to learn a new way of thinking, feeling and living; a way of seeing through the mirage of my stress, resentment and assumption to a politics that was less about blame and more about finding common ground. And I had to do this even if it meant becoming an outcast from my own community.

All my life a sense of powerlessness had followed me around. I was powerless to read a book, powerless to enjoy poetry and powerless to get a job. I was powerless to leave unhealthy toxic relationships, powerless over junk food and powerless to stop drinking and taking drugs. My answer to every instance in which I lacked power was to demand that someone else intervene on my behalf: junk food should be curtailed, advertising should be restricted and alcohol and drugs should be banned. I dreamed of society imploding, naively believing demise would make life easier. Everything was immoral, unjust and tinged with corruption. Worse still, I believed those things so vehemently that it would emotionally disturb and offend me to hear someone argue to the contrary. Turns out that was a very foolish way to burn energy. But it's often much easier to see the holes in another person's story than it is to get honest about the yarns you've been spinning.

As I sit here in Starbucks, on the burial ground of my teenage ideals, I am struck by a comforting sense that life may not be so bad. The Pollok Free State, rather than becoming a distant memory, lives on in the GalGael Trust, run by Colin Macleod's widow and fellow environmentalist Gehan Macleod. The GalGael is a successful local community project that 'serves as something of a safe harbour for those whose lives have been battered by storms such as worklessness, depression or addiction.'

Based in Govan, they offer a workplace that challenges, inspires and creates the conditions conducive to learning; a space where mistakes are not only made but owned as our best teachers, where old issues are left at the door and new identities forged. Their whole ethos is about encouraging people to take responsibility for their lives and move beyond adversity.

The young socialists who were demoralised by the collapse of their movement in the mid-'90s are now influential activists, trade unionists, journalists and community leaders who subtly direct the national debate on a variety of issues – human rights, equality and, of course, poverty. Over in Castlemilk, Cathy didn't get elected but the experience of running a campaign proved invaluable and CAA continues to grow, based on its ethos of political participation and self-determination.

And last week, my sister, despite all of the difficulties she has faced so far in life, got accepted to Glasgow University to study politics – the first person in our family to do so.

Today, as I try to get these last few hundred words down before my son wakes up from his nap, I'm forced to confront the once unthinkable notion that society, while riddled with internal contradiction, may not be so cruel, callous or beyond my control as I once believed. Acknowledging this is not a slight on those who struggle. I am overwhelmed by gratitude that the society in which I just happened to be born, despite all its glaring injustices and vast room for improvement, has retained enough of its basic integrity that I was able to overcome my personal difficulties and lead a more honest and useful life. Now with a child to raise, the thought of a revolution frightens me. Young activists seem self-righteous and unreasonable. Social movements appear far too keen to placate any and all forms of anger in order to grow their support, with little thought given to the usefulness of much of the anger beyond its function as a political battering ram. When I look at the left, I see a worrying lack of self-awareness and a pathological belief in the legitimacy of our own resentment which is beginning to undermine the broader objective of social justice. I see working class people who don't suit the agenda being written off by the activists, artists and politicians that are supposed to defend and inspire them. And worst of all, I get the sense that views like mine are increasingly unwelcome. Sometimes I feel the left is no longer a safe place for someone like me. But I've been wrong before. Either way, this arouses instincts in me I never knew I had, which are about protecting my own family and preserving my son's quality of life. This next phase, as I approach middle age, will be about reconciling the new reality of my life as a responsible parent with the idealism of my past. No doubt these words may horrify many of you. Especially those who thought this book would be calling for a revolution or assumed I would use it to pin the blame for poverty on one political party. If this is the case, then I am sorry to disappoint.

That was the old me. I'm different now. Who knows, maybe allowing myself to evolve is a betrayal of my class or a renunciation of my heritage. Perhaps it's blasphemous to imply that we, as individuals and communities, must accept a level of responsibility for the way we think, feel and live and that a society built along any other lines is not worth having. Perhaps that's giving in and submitting. Perhaps that's selling out. It's really not for me to say, is it? What I can say is that it would be a far greater betrayal of myself and my community to deny or conceal the fact that, despite my best efforts, I have changed. That, is the most radical thing a person can do.

Luath Press Limited

committed to publishing well written books worth reading

LUATH PRESS takes its name from Robert Burns, whose little collie Luath (*Gael.*, swift or nimble) tripped up Jean Armour at a wedding and gave him the chance to speak to the woman who was to be his wife and the abiding love of his life. Burns called one of the 'Twa Dogs' Luath after Cuchullin's hunting dog in Ossian's *Fingal*. Luath Press was established in 1981 in the heart of Burns country, and is now based a few steps up the road from Burns' first lodgings on Edinburgh's Royal Mile. Luath offers you distinctive writing with a hint of unexpected pleasures.

Most bookshops in the UK, the US, Canada, Australia, New Zealand and parts of Europe, either carry our books in stock or can order them for you. To order direct from us, please send a £sterling cheque, postal order, international money order or your credit card details (number, address of cardholder and expiry date) to us at the address below. Please add post and packing as follows: UK – £1.00 per delivery address; overseas surface mail – £2.50 per delivery address; overseas airmail – £3.50 for the first book to each delivery address, plus £1.00 for each additional book by airmail to the same address. If your order is a gift, we will happily enclose your card or message at no extra charge. .

Luath Press Limited
543/2 Castlehill
The Royal Mile
Edinburgh EH1 2ND
Scotland
Telephone: +44 (0)131 225 4326 (24 hours)
email: sales@luath. co.uk
Website: www. luath.co.uk